COUNTY FOLK-LORE
Printed extracts no. 2.

SUFFOLK

Fascimile reprint
Llanerch/FLS
Felinfach, 1997

ISBN 1 86143 033 7

Issued by THE FOLK-LORE SOCIETY.]

COUNTY FOLK-LORE.

PRINTED EXTRACTS No. 2.

SUFFOLK.

Collected and edited
by
The Lady Eveline Camilla Gurdon
with introduction
by
Edward Clodd

Fascimile reprint
Llanerch/FLS
Felinfach, 1997

ISBN 1 86143 033 7

Published for the Folk-Lore Society by
D. NUTT, 270, STRAND, W.C.
J. LODER, WOODBRIDGE.
PAWSEY & HAYES, IPSWICH.

1893.

Alter et Idem.

The Folklore Society, original publishers of this book, was founded in 1878 and was the first learned society in the world to be devoted to the study of folklore. Its expressed aims were to encourage research and collection of traditional culture, and to make the results of this research available to scholars and the public at large.

The Society is still going strong, and organises regular conferences and other events, issues a well-respected journal and members' newsletter, publishes books on folklore topics, and maintains an extensive library and archive service which is based in University College London. Membership is open to anyone interested in furthering the Society's aims.

Information regarding the Society's activities and current subscription rates is available from The Folklore Society, University College London, Gower Street, London WC1E 6BT (Tel 071 387 5894).

INTRODUCTION

The word "folklore" was invented almost 150 years ago, on August 22 1846, when the antiquarian W. J. Thoms appealed in the *Athenæum* for readers to join in recording"... what we in England designate as Popular Antiquities or Popular Literature (though by-the-by it is more a Lore than a Literature, and would be most aptly described by a good Saxon compound, Folk-lore) ...". The word was new, but the subject was not; for two hundred years antiquarians had been fascinated by local and seasonal customs, popular tales, traditions, beliefs which did not conform to official relligion or science. Such material appears sporadically in the writings of William Camden (1551-1623), and far more abundantly in those of John Aubrey (1626-97). Some decades later came Henry Bourne's *Antiquitates Vulgares* (1725), a fierce attack against popular relligious observances such as Christmas carols or visiting holy wells, because they were originally Roman Catholic, "the invention of indolent monks", and so undoubtedly diabolical and heathen. His book, ignored at the time, was incorporated in 1777 into a much larger and more influential work, John Brand's *Observations on Popular Antiquities*. Brand agreed that most folk customs dated from before the Reformation, but he was free from the Puritan intolerance which equated Catholicism with paganism, and he enjoyed historical research for its own sake. He went on gathering material till his death in 1806, mostly by copying from books and journals, but sometimes by personal observation. After he died, his book was reissued in a greatly enlarged edition, incorporating the later notes by Henry Ellis (1815). It had grown into a vast, confused scrapbook: local historians pounced upon it and used it as a model for their own researches.

In the course of the nineteenth century, many

1

scholars boldly tried to formulate some all-embracing theory which would explain the origin and significance of myths, folktales, superstitions and magical beliefs, and the more picturesque folk customs, especially those connected with agriculture. The explanations offered went far beyond medieval Catholicism. Some suggested origins in pre-Christian Germanic or Celtic cultures; others, noting similarities with beliefs and rituals found among "primitive" non-European peoples, argued that folklore consisted of survivals from a prehistoric "savage" stage in human social development. The debate between these and other conflicting theories was carried on energetically at a high scholarly level, and attracted much public interest. It has been well described in Richard M. Dorson's The British Folklorists: A History (1968). And although modern scholars agree that all these Victorian attempts to find "a key to all mythologies" ended in failure, due to over-simplifications of the highly complex topics, some of the theories then launched are still to be found recycled in popular form: prehistoric paganism and Celtic paganism, separately or combined, are currently enjoying a fashionable revival in the mass market.

By the 1890s the Folklore Society, which had been founded in 1878, saw a need for systematic and accurate documentation of traditions within specific localities: huge unwieldy compilations like Brand's would not do. Between 1895 and 1914 seven volumes of County Folklore: Printed Extracts were published by the Society. The first covered three counties: Gloucestershire by E. S. Hartland, Suffolk by Lady Carilla Eveline Gurdon, and Leicestershire and Rutland by C. J. Billson. The rest covered one region apiece: The North Riding of Yorkshire, York, and the Ainsty by Eliza Gutch; Orkney and Shetland Islands by George Black, and ed. N. W. Thomas; Northumberland by M. C. ·Balfour and N. W. Thomas; Lincolnshire by Eliza

Gutch and Mabel Peacock; The East Riding of York-shire by Eliza Gutch; and Fife by J. E. Simpkins. The 1914 war then interrupted the project.

These books may seem strange today because, like Brand's, they consist almost entirely of extracts from previously printed books and journals. Fieldwork, i.e. gathering information through interviews or by tape-recording, filming, and personal observation, is central to a present-day folklorist's technique, and was already practised in Victorian times by means of the simple notebook. Yet from these books it is virtually absent; editorial theorising and interpretation are also minimal. It must be stressed that the "Printed Extracts" series was never intended to stand alone, but to be a starting point for further study of the contemporary lore of each area. In his preface to the Gloucestershire vol-ume, Hartland made "suggestions for systematic col-lection of folklore" to be undertaken by university students, school teachers, clergy, doctors, local his-torians and others. Plenty of his contemporaries were already working in this way; the purpose of reprinting old material was to provide historical perspectives and a set of securely dated benchmarks, from which to measure later developments, innovations or loses.

Another century has passed, and the County Folk-lore series is being reprinted in the 1990s, a period of nostalgia for an idealized rural past, seen as a time of idyllic simplicity and closeness to nature. Readers will find ample encouragement for nostalgia here - pictur-esque accounts of harvest customs, Christmas customs, fairs and festivals; old tales of ghosts, giants, fairies, boggarts, witches, heroes, bandits, healing charms, divinations, omens, spells; customs at marriage, birth or death. It is only too easy to see in all this mere quaintness and charm. To get a more historically bal-anced picture one needs to remember also the harsh social and economic conditions affecting very many rural workers: one may well wonder, for instance, whether a good harvest supper really compensated for low wages during the other 51 weeks of the year. The "printed extracts", like old photographs, offer facts – but facts selected and presented according to the viewpoint of the observers who recorded them. Now, in the 1990s, we inevitably add interpretative viewpoints of our own, conditioned by the cultural assumptions of our age.

Folklore is an ongoing process, in which every custom, story or belief (if it survives) is constantly re-modelled by social pressures so that it remains in some way relevant to changing conditions. Books written a hundred or two hundred years ago are in no sense a final word on the topic, nor are the versions of a story or custom which they contain necessarily "better" than the current ones – they merely pinpoint what it was like in one phase of its existence. Moreover, anything that is passed on through oral tradition exists in multiple versions, each differing in some degree from the next, and each equally valid. What is the "true" story about that haunted tree? What is the "right" way to dispose of Christmas decorations, and on what date? What "should" children do at Halloween? Are black cats lucky (UK), or unlucky (USA)? We shall never find definitive answers to such questions, but it is fascinating to compile our own observations about them, and to compare with writers who went hunting along the same tracks long before us.

Jacqueline Simpson,
President,
The Folklore Society,
February, 1994.

CONTENTS.

AUTHORITIES.

Aubrey, John. "Miscellanies upon Various Subjects." By John Aubrey, Esq., F.R.S. London : Printed for W. Ottridge, Strand ; and E. Easton, at Salisbury. 1784.

Brand, John. "Observations on Popular Antiquities." London : C. Knight & Co., 22, Ludgate Street. 1842.

Camden, W. "Britain," translated by Philemon Holland. London. 1637.

Chambers, R. "The Book of Days." W. and R. Chambers, London and Edinburgh. 1864.

Choice Notes. (Folk-lore from "Notes and Queries.") 1889.

Cullum, Rev. Sir John, Bart. "History and Antiquities of Hawstead and Hardwick." 2nd edition. London : Printed for and by Nichols, Son, and Bentley, Red Lion Passage, Fleet Street. 1813.

Dickens, Charles. "The Personal History of David Copperfield." London : Chapman & Hall.

East Anglian (*The*) ; or, "Notes and Queries." Edited by Samuel Tymms. Lowestoft : S. Tymms, 60, High Street. 1869.

East Anglian (*The*); or, "Notes and Queries." New Series. Edited by C. H. Evelyn White. Ipswich : Pawsey & Hayes, Ancient House (1885 to present date).

FitzGerald, Edward. *Works*. (Houghton, Mifflin & Co.'s Edition.) 1887.

Forby, Rev. Robert. "The Vocabulary of East Anglia." London : J. B. Nichols & Son, 25, Parliament Street. 1830.

Gage, John. "History and Antiquities of Hengrave." London : J. Carpenter, Old Bond Street. 1822. "History and Antiquities of Suffolk," Thingoe Hundred. Deck, Bury St. Edmunds. 1838.

Glyde, John. "The New Suffolk Garland." Ipswich : Printed for the Author, St. Matthew's Street. London : Simpkin, Marshall & Co. 1866.

Groome, F. Hindes. An Article called "A Suffolk Parson," in Blackwood's Edinburgh Magazine of March, 1891. W. Blackwood & Sons, 45, George Street, Edinburgh.

Grose, F. "Antiquities of England and Wales."

Hele, N. F. "Notes or Jottings about Aldeburgh." 2nd Edition. 1890.

Hazlitt, W. Carew. " English Proverbs and Proverbial Phrases," arranged and annotated. J. Russell Smith, 36, Soho Square, London. 1869.

Hollingsworth, Rev. A. " History of Stowmarket." Ipswich : Pawsey, Old Butter Market. 1844.

Hone, William. " The Everyday Book and Table Book." Year Book, in three vols. London : Printed for Thomas Tegg, 73, Cheapside. 1826.

Martin, T. " History of Thetford." London : J. Nichols. 1779.

Moor, Ed. " Oriental Fragments." London : Smith, Elder & Co., Cornhill. 1834.

Moor, Ed. " Suffolk Words and Phrases." Woodbridge : J. Loder. 1823.

Murray, John. " Handbook for Essex, Suffolk, Norfolk, and Cambridgeshire." 2nd Edition. J. Murray, Albermarle Street. 1875.

Nall, John Greaves. " Chapters on the East Anglian Coast." Longmans & Co. 1866.

Raven, J. J., D.D. " The Church Bells of Suffolk." London : Jarrold & Sons.

Ray, J. " A Complete Collection of English Proverbs." London : W. Ottridge. 1768.

Scott, Sir Walter, Bart. " Demonology and Witchcraft." London : G. Routledge & Son. 1807.

Shakespeare, William. " K. Henry VI."

Suffolk Garland (The); or, " East Country Minstrel." Ipswich : Printed and sold by John Raw ; sold also by Longman, Hurst, Rees, Orme & Brown ; and Rodd & Son, London. 1818.

Suffolk Notes and Queries. Ipswich Journal. 1877.

Tryal of Witches (A) at the Assizes at Bury St. Edmonds, 10th March, 1664, before Sir M. Hale. Taken by a Person then attending the Court. London : Printed for W. Shrewsbery, at the Bible, in Duck Lane. 1682.

Tusser, Thomas. " Five Hundred Points of Good Husbandry." Edited by W. Mavor. London : Printed for Lackington, Allen & Co., Temple of the Muses, Finsbury Square, by Harding & Wright, St. John's Square. 1812.

Varden, John T. " Chapter on Traditions, Superstitions, and Folk-lore " in the " East Anglian Handbook and Agricultural Annual for 1885." Norwich : *Argus* Office, St. Giles.

Zincke, The Rev. F. B. " Some materials for the History of Wherstead," published by Read and Barrett, Ipswich. 1887.

INTRODUCTION.

THE extracts from printed sources, more or less available, together with a few additions from oral testimony, which the skill and industry of Lady Camilla Gurdon have gathered in the following pages, are further justification for the action of our Council in the dis-interring of local records of customs, superstitious beliefs, and aught else included within the psychical department of the Science of Man known as "Folk-Lore."

The value of the material thus collected lies in what may be called its achromatism. It comes to us unrefracted through the prism of prejudice or pre-conceived theories, bringing before us "the things commonly believed" among the folk, gentle as well as simple, into whose minds no doubt or question as to *whether* the thing was, only as to *when* and *how* it was, ever entered. It is, to change the comparison, from such rich ore as these old deposits of primary thought supply, that the folk-lorist may smelt the material which discloses the history of its origin and formation.

A glance at the section-headings of this Collection shows that Suffolk—and it is not pretended that the whole county

has been ransacked—has proved richer in such deposits than
might, *prima facie*, have been expected.   The Rev. R.
Forby, in his valuable *Vocabulary of East Anglia*, published
in 1830, speaks of the absence of weird and gloomy legends
and other elements of the "poetry of superstition" in the
counties of Norfolk and Suffolk, and attributes this partly
to the level and monotonous nature of a county whose tame
features, instead of feeding belief in the spirits and demons
and ogres of mountains, caves, valleys and torrential streams,
created the gentler types, the helpful or spiteful "little folk,"
the housewifely-fairy, the walking ghost of haunted halls
and manor-houses, and the wise women who injured the
cattle.   A second reason assigned by Mr. Forby for paucity
of materials is the stern fanaticism which marked the people
of East Anglia two centuries ago.   They were "the first
to associate in support of the Parliament against King Charles,
and the principles of Puritanism prevailed among them for
many years in their utmost rigour.   It is scarcely necessary
to say that the Puritans abhorred and proscribed every
superstition but their own, which consisted principally in
a firm belief in witchcraft."   Forby adds that this belief
is, in fact, "the only really popular and prevailing instance
of superstition existing among us."*   Puritanism, starting
as a revolt against the ceremonial of a State Church, became,
in the nature of things, a revolt against ecclesiastical
authority, and an assertion of the supreme authority of
Scripture, which involved unquestioning belief in everything
found within its four corners ; therefore belief in witchcraft.

* *l.c.* II. 388.

In this the Puritans were neither inconsistent nor singular. In 1665, Sir Matthew Hale, trying two women for witchcraft, said: "That there are such creatures as witches, I make no doubt at all, for the Scriptures have affirmed so much,"[*] and a century later, when the laws against witchcraft, which had lain dormant for many years, had been repealed,[†] John Wesley wrote in his journal: "the giving up witchcraft is in effect giving up the Bible."[‡] With the old belief—the equal value of the component parts of Scripture—such contention was not to be·gainsaid. But with the purblindness which cannot see that although "there are diversities of operations," the essence of supernal agency must be the same, the Puritans compounded for beliefs

> "they were inclined to
> By damning those they had no mind to,"

hence the force of Mr. Forby's remark that, "they abhorred and proscribed every superstition but their own." "Naturam expellas furca, tamen usque recurret," which we may freely translate: "you may expel superstition with a pitchfork, but it will come back between the prongs;" and despite the activity of Puritanism (of which, as of Dissent generally, East Anglia was once the great stronghold), in repressing what it looked on as "old wives' fables," the inherited and persistent beliefs were passed on in secret through beldam to beldam from generation to generation, and are yet held as "gospel truth" in many a bye-nook of Suffolk. The history

---

[*] Cf. Deut. xviii. 10 ; 1 Sam. xxviii. 7, 8 ; 2 Chron. xxiii. 6, etc.
[†] By 10 George II. 1736.
[‡] Cf. Exodus xx. 18.

of the decline in the belief in witchcraft, as in other forms of Satanic activity, shows that illusions and falsities are not killed either by argument or repression ; they die of inanition when changes to which they cannot adapt themselves occur in the intellectual or spiritual atmosphere. In connection with this subject, which occupies so large a space in the extracts, special thanks are due to Lady Camilla Gurdon for unearthing the details of the trial of Amy Duny and Rose Callender at Lowestoft (*vid. infra*, pp. 194—199). It was just observed that, however varied the form of belief in the action of supernatural causes, the substance is the same; and in reading the extracts in which, for example, magic is seen to play so large a part, its difference from witchcraft seems to consist only in this: that while the one is due to direct personal action and influence, the other is due to impersonal agencies and remote or less direct influences. The large number of examples given on pp. 14—17; 19—21; 26, 30, 31, 193, 201, come under the head of " sympathetic magic " or belief in interaction due to superficial correspondences, which is an universal note of barbaric thought; and their presence would call for special comment, did we not meet at every turn with evidence that we have but to scratch the rustic to find the barbarian underneath. Mr. Frazer's *Golden Bough* and Prof. Jevons's Introduction to Plutarch's *Romane Questions* may be consulted with advantage in this connection, while to their numerous references may be added that given by Prof. Burnet to the numbers of Pythagoras. " 33. When you rise from the bedclothes, roll them together, and smooth out the impress of the body ; " the reason being that some evil-disposed person might stick pins in the impress.*

Very interesting also are the additions to the folk-lore of medicine supplied by cures and charms, and by the barely extinct (*vid.* p. 28) practice of passing sickly or deformed children through a cleft ash, which tree, it will be remembered, was held only second to the oak as a sacred object by the "Aryan"-speaking races of Europe, and, like the oak, was probably worshipped by an older race. The examples of that wide-spread custom of "telling the bees" when the death of a member of the family occurs, embodying the pretty and touching idea of community between the owner and his possessions, suggests reference to the still extant custom along the East Coast (which, I think, is known on the Cornish coast also), of putting a ship "in mourning" when her owner dies by painting a narrow blue streak round her. The decay of private ship-owners is fatal to the continuance of a custom which has a touch of poetry and of the old communistic idea in it, the personality of a ship being keenly felt by all connected with her, and the more so when, as often happened, she was, at her christening, named after the owner, his wife, or child.

While upon this topic I will further digress in the hope of obtaining additional information from students of customs which may throw light upon the origin of the still existing practice, in cases of private partnerships in vessels, of dividing the shares into sixty-fourths. The following

* *Early Greek Philosophy*, p. 104.

extract from a letter from my friend the Hon. John Abercromby, after a visit made by him to Sweden and Denmark, throws some light on the matter:—

"I promised to try to find out for you if the Scandinavians knew of any such custom. I regret to say that all my enquiries resulted in a shake of the head, and a muttered 'I never heard of it.' But though I could learn nothing from my informants, mostly captains of steamers, I think I have a clue to the mystery. In the Viking ship preserved at Christiania I counted 16 oars on each side. If they worked in double shifts this would give a crew of 64 rowers. As you are aware, the stones over a grave in the Viking period are sometimes arranged in the form of a ship with rows to mark the benches. There is one figured in a *Guide to Northern Archæology, by the Royal Soc. of North. Antiq.*, Copenhagen, edited by the Earl of Ellesmere (1848, p. 34), with 16 banks of oars."

In his *Village Community*, Mr. Gomme, basing his information on the authority of Mr. Hodgson, cites as a "typical example of the village community in India," the "existence of two classes of villagers : the original settlers or their descendants, and strangers not descended from original settlers. . . . The privileges of the original settlers are held by custom in four principal shares, and each principal share is subdivided into sixteen parts, making in all sixty-four shares." * Assuming that the ships of sea-roving folk were, like the lands of village communities, originally tribal, would not this explain the origin of a custom whose existence to this day is one of the most interesting examples of survival?

The extract from Major Moor's scarce *Oriental Fragments* describing the procession of the white bull at Bury St. Edmunds (p. 124) is an useful addition to Mr. Gomme's remarks on this matter in his last Presidential Address ; †

* *l.c.* p. 32.   † *Folk-Lore*, March, 1893, p. 9.

and in the adornment of the last sheaf at harvest-time with a green bough (p. 69), we have an example of a custom as to the practice of which, incited by Mr. Frazer's references to it in the *Golden Bough*, Lady Camilla Gurdon made numerous enquiries in South-East Suffolk.

The variety of the extracts tempts one to continue comments which, however, must have an end, especially as with the completion of the work of collection throughout the counties of Great Britain and Ireland, the classification of the material will follow, and its relative value and significance be made apparent. But that desired conclusion will not be reached for many a day.

The List of Authorities whence the following extracts are derived far from represent the books which Lady Camilla Gurdon has examined, and in many of which nothing bearing on the folk-lore of the county has been found. Her Ladyship wisely supplemented these labours by enquiries of old and young, gardeners, schoolgirls, and others, from whom a fair amount of corroborative matter has been gathered. Special thanks are due to Miss Nina Layard for the collection of games printed on pp. 62—66, and to Mr. Redstone, English master in the Grammar School at Woodbridge, the frequent occurrence of whose name at the foot of communications attests the services which he has rendered.

Lady Camilla Gurdon will permit me, in the name of the Council of the Folk-Lore Society, to express their deep obligations to herself, and to add their thanks to Miss Layard and Mr. Redstone.

EDWARD CLODD.

EXAMPLES

TRADITIONS ALREADY RECORDED.

I.—AGRICULTURAL MYTHS.

Weeds. . . . I have heard confidently announced as if there could be no doubt about it, that weeds are natural to the ground, in the sense that the ground originates them ; and that no man ever did, because no man ever could, eradicate them. They spring eternal from the ground itself, not at all necessarily from the seeds of parent weeds. . . . To this ignorance is superadded in the case of weeds a theological conception, that the ground has been cursed with weeds as a punishment for man's disobedience. It has therefore ever borne, and will ever continue to bear, for the punishment of the husbandman (but why should husbandmen only be punished), thistles and poppies and speargrass. It is then useless, not to say that it is a sign of a rebellious spirit, to attempt to clean one's land thoroughly. It is pious to accept this dispensation up to a certain point.

"Some materials for the Hist. of Wherstead," by F.
B. Zincke, p. 178.

Stones.—I was some years ago assured by an educated farmer who had much intelligence, and who took in a weekly paper, that it was of no manner of use to have stones picked off one's land (I have heard the same opinion expressed by others) because—this was the reason he gave—it is an undoubted fact that the land produces them. He insisted that this assertion of his was not only in accordance with the order of nature, because everything, even a stone, must have been produced, but was also a result of his own experience ; for he had several times had the stones picked off a certain field, and now there were upon it as many as ever.

Ibid. p. 178.

A man at Martlesham had placed upon his window-sill a conglomeration of pebbles (Pudding-Stone). He told Mr. Redstone that it was a Mother-Stone. He believed it to be the parent of the pebbles.

From Mr. Redstone, Woodbridge.

Primroses.—At Cockfield, Suffolk, there are none, nor, it is said, do they thrive when planted, though they are numerous in all the surrounding villages, which do not apparently differ from Cockfield in soil.

The village legend says that here, too, they once were plentiful, but when Cockfield was depopulated by the plague, they also caught the infection and died, nor have they flourished since that time.—E.G.R. (Vol. VII., p. 201.)

Choice Notes (Folklore from *Notes and Queries*), 1889. The vols. refer to Notes and Queries.

Virgin Mary Thistle.—The beautiful and magnificent *Carduus Benedictus,* or Blessed Thistle. Its broad bright leaves are marked with white well defined spots, as if they had held milk. Our popular legend . . . is that Our Lady, when thirsty, met with a cow ; and being at a loss for a vessel for receiving the milk, perceived this species of thistle—but not then variegated—at hand, and using its broad leaf as a convenient cup, she willed that the species should, as a grateful testimony of its well-timed utility, ever indelibly retain the marks it then received from its useful application ; and bear also the name of its pure patroness.

Edward Moor. "Suffolk Words and Phrases," p. 456.

Natur.—Providence—destiny. "Con-*tra*-ry"—strongly accenting the medial—"to natur." I was trying to explain to rather an intelligent farmer, how lightening was brought from a cloud, as practised by Franklin and others, but he was shocked at the impiety of the attempt, saying it was "contrary to natur."

Ed. Moor. "Suffolk Words and Phrases," p. 245.

St. Edmund's Day (20th Nov.)—

> Set garlike and beans at St. Edmond the King,
> The moon in the wane, thereon hangeth a thing :
>   Th' encrease of a pottle (well proved of some),
>   Shall pleasure thy household, ere peascod time come.

Thomas Tusser. "Five Hundred points of Good Husbandry," p. 49.

> Set garlic and pease,
> Saint Edmond to please.

Thomas Tusser. "Five Hundred points of Good Husbandry," p. 43.

Pudduck.—A toad . . . we, in common with Shakespeare, believe that spiders and toads "suck the poison" of the earth—a sentiment put into the fine speech of Richard II. on his landing in England—

> — Weeping, smiling, greet I thee, my earth :
> Feed not thy Sovereign's foes my gentle earth ;
>   But let thy spiders that suck up thy venom,
>   And heavy gaited toads, lie in their way.
>
> Richard II, Act III, Sc. 2.

Ed. Moor. "Suffolk Words and Phrases," p. 295.

Snake-spit.—Small masses of delicately white frothy matter* seen on leaves of weeds or wild flowers, in the spring mostly, popularly believed to be the saliva of snakes . . . *Frog-spit* and *toad-spittle* are other names for this froth, the origin of which has considerably puzzled rustic . . . philosophers.

Ibid. p. 369

* A secretion of larva of *Aphrophora spumaria.*

Howslick.—The house leek. *Sempervivum tectorum*—frequently seen on cottage roofs. This is a very ancient usage, as defensative against lightening.

Ed. Moor. "Suffolk Words and Phrases," p. 177.

Thunder Pipe. — *Thunder-bolt* — *Thunder-pic* — or *Thunder-stone.* Lithic cylinders, or frustra of cones, two or three inches long, and about the thickness of a black lead pencil, are so called; and are picked up and looked on with some reverence among us. The true sort are straight, and are, I believe, classed by naturalists among the *Brontiae* or *Belemnites.* But generally, most small stones of a cylindrical form are called by one of these names. We fancy some of them fall in thunderstorms . . . Shakespeare has the word and feeling as in Suffolk—

> Fear no more the lightening-flash
> Nor the all-dread thunderstone.
>
> Cymbeline, IV, 1.

> I have bared my bosom to the thunderstone.
> Jul. Cæsar, I, 2.

Ibid. p. 431.

The Cross was made of Elder-wood. — Speaking to some little children one day about the danger of taking shelter under trees during a thunderstorm, one of them said that it was not so with all trees, 'for,' said he, 'you will be quite safe under an *eldern* tree, because the Cross was made of that, and so the lightning never strikes it.'

Mushrooms will not grow after they have been seen.

Suffolk. C. W. J., "Book of Days," vol. ii, p. 322.

II.—ANIMAL OMENS.

The Raven.—The belief that a visit, accompanied with a croak, from a raven bodes the approaching death of one of the family is as general here as elsewhere. . . . In my early time in Suffolk, while I was living at Freston, there was a pair which bred year after year in the contiguous parish of Woolverstone, in a lofty oak between the Hall and the river. One day my housekeeper, with faltering voice and distressful look, told me of having that morning been wholly knocked down by hearing and seeing the fateful visitor. As was natural, it did not occur to her that the visit and croak could have had any reference to herself; and so she thought it her duty—which, however, she was very loth to discharge—to inform me of what was in store for myself.

> "Some materials for the Hist. of Wherstead," by F.
> B. Zincke, p. 171.

Bees.—As late as my early time here it was still the practice, when a death occurred in a house where bees were kept, for some members of the family to go to the bees and tap them; and when the bees came out, to whisper to them the loss the family had sustained. The supposition here was that, because the bees showed so much intelligence and were so industrious, they must be regarded as partners with or members of the family, and were entitled to the information that one of those for whom and with whom they were working was gone. It was believed that if they were not duly apprised of these events they would resent the neglect by making no more honey, or even by leaving the place. I knew a case in this parish where the owner of the hives, not being content with informing the bees of the death that had occurred, was in the habit of putting them into mourning; this she did by placing round each hive a band of crape. . . .

Another superstition about bees I fell in with while establishing an apiary, now many years ago, was the old and wide-spread one that they were not to be paid for with money. This originated in the same idea as the practice just noticed. Their intelligence and industry entitled them to be treated as members of the family —at all events, should save them from being bought and sold like cattle.

Ibid. p. 170.

They (bees) are said to be so sensitive as to leave houses, the inmates of which indulge habitually in swearing.

"The New Suffolk Garland," p. 172.

It is unlucky that a stray swarm of bees should settle on your premises, unclaimed by their owner.

Going to my father's house one day I found the household in a state of excitement, as a stray swarm had settled on the pump. The coachman and I hived them securely . . . I was saying that they might think themselves fortunate in getting a hive of bees so cheap; but . . . one man employed about the premises looked very grave and shook his head . . . he told me in a solemn undertone that he did not mean to say there was anything in it, but people *did* say that if a stray swarm of bees came to a house, and were not claimed by their owner, there would be a death in the family within the year. . . .

Bees will not thrive if you quarrel about them.

I was congratulating a parishioner on her bees looking so well, and at the same time expressing my surprise that her next-door neighbour's hives, which had formerly been so prosperous, now seemed quite deserted. 'Ah!' she answered, 'them bees couldn't du . . . there was words about them, and bees'll niver du if there's words about them.' . . .

. . . . A neighbour of mine had bought a hive of bees at an auction of the goods of a farmer who had recently died. The bees seemed very sickly and not likely to thrive, when my neighbour's servant bethought him that they had never been put in mourning for their late master; on this he got a piece of crape and tied it to a stick, which he fastened to the hive. After this the bees recovered, . . . a result which was unhesitatingly attributed to their having been put into mourning.

Suffolk.   C. W. J., "Book of Days," vol. i, p. 752.

Robins.—'You must not take robin's eggs; if you do you will get your legs broken,' is the saying in Suffolk. And accordingly you will never find their eggs on the long strings of which boys are so proud.

Their lives too are generally respected. 'It is unlucky to kill a robin.' 'How badly you write,' I said one day to a boy in our parish school; 'your hand shakes so that you can't hold the pen steady. Have you been running hard, or anything of that sort?' 'No,' replied the lad, 'it always shakes; I once had a robin die in my hand; and they say that if a robin dies in your hand, it will always shake.'

The belief in ill-luck through bringing small birds' eggs into a house is widespread in E. Anglia.

Various.—The cross on the donkey's back is still connected in the rustic mind with our Lord's having ridden upon one into Jerusalem on Palm Sunday. . . .

It is lucky for you if martins should build against your house, for they never come to one where there is strife. . . .

It is unlucky to count lambs before a certain time; if you do, they will be sure not to thrive. . . .

It is unlucky to kill a '*harvest man*,' i.e. one of those long-legged spiders which one sees scrambling about perfectly independent of cobwebs; if you do kill one there will be a bad harvest.

. . . The poor hedgehog finds to his cost that the absurd notion of his sucking the teats of cows serves as a pretext for the most cruel treatment.

It is currently believed that if you put horse-hairs into a spring they will turn to eels. A few months ago, a labouring man told a friend of mine that 'he knew it was so, for he had proved it.' He had put a number of horse-hairs into a spring near his house, and in a short time it was full of young eels. . . .

The saying about magpies is well-known—

> ' One, sorrow ;
> Two, mirth ;
> Three, a wedding ;
> Four, death.'

Suffolk, C. W. J. *Ibid.* vol. i, p. 678.

Bishop-Barnabee, s. the pretty insect more generally called the Lady-bird or May-bug, *Coccinella septem punctata,* Lin. It is one of those few highly favoured among God's harmless creatures, which superstition protects from wanton injury. Some obscurity hangs over this popular name of it. . . . The name has most probably been derived from the Barn-Bishop ; whether in scorn of that silly and profane mockery, or in pious commemoration of it, must depend on the time of its adoption, before or since the Reformation. . . .

Forby. " Vocab. of E. Anglia," vol. i, p. 26.

The booming of the bittern in places which it does not usually frequent, forebodes a rise in the price of wheat.

Rooks building near a house are a sign of prosperity.

A horse is believed to have the power of seeing ghosts ; this is probably derived from the account of Balaam's ass discerning the angel.

The howling of dogs is a sign of ill-luck.

Crickets betoken good luck to the house they inhabit, and if they quit the house suddenly it is a very bad omen.

Ibid. vol. ii, appendix.

> The robin red-breast and the wren
> Are God Almighty's cock and hen ;
> The martin and the swallow
> Are the next two birds that follow.
> Old Adage.

. . . The superstitious dread of killing or hurting any of them still continues in full force . . . The martin in particular is believed to bring good luck to the house on which it builds its nest.

Ibid. vol. ii, p. 409.

If a pregnant woman meets a hare, and turns it back, the child will have a hare lip, but if she allows it to pass her, no harm will happen to her.

"The New Suffolk Garland," p. 177.

Pullet's Eggs.—"Them there little eggs is cock's eggs, an' if you was to hatch 'em, a cockytrice would come out. Tha's a sort o' sarpent."

A. W. T., "Suffolk Notes and Queries," Ipswich Journal, 1877.

Mr. Redstone has known people who have objected to sleeping on a feather bed, and women who have refused to be confined upon one for fear lest there should be dow's (dove's) feather's in it, in which case if they died upon it, they would die hard.

From Mr. Redstone.

Lucky Bee.—A humble, or as *we* say, a *Bumble-bee*, got out to sea, quite from his latitude, and welcomed as a bringer of good luck, if he alight on board. He is not always so tenderly used ashore, by the boys at any rate, who, chasing him for his honey, as I was told, would pull him in two directly he was caught, " *lest he should eat up his own honey,*" if he got the chance.

Ed. FitzGerald. " E. Anglian or Notes and Queries," edited by S. Tymms, vol. iv, p. 263.

Butter-fly.—Considered lucky, and therefore tenderly entreated when straying into house or net-chamber. I am told by a learned Professor that the same belief prevails in India.

Ed. FitzGerald. *Ibid.* vol. iv, p. 110.

Do you remember an old rhyme which I certainly have heard in Suffolk . . . it runs thus :— . . .

> "If the Slow-worm could see and the Viper could hear,
> Then England from Serpents would never be clear."

Or thus :—

> "If the Viper could hear and the Slow-worm could see,
> Then England from Serpents would never be free."

I want to quote it and cannot be certain which is the proper form.

E. FitzGerald. *Ibid.* vol. ii, p. 118.

III.—BIRTH CUSTOMS.

Custom at the Birth of a Child.—There is an extraordinary notion in regard to the birth of children. As soon as they are born they ought, it is said, to be carried . UP stairs,* or they will never *rise* to riches and distinction in their after life, and accordingly, if there are no attics for the nurse to climb up into, she will sometimes mount upon a chair or stool with the new-born baby in her arms.

"The New Suffolk Garland," p. 177.

Pin-basket, s. the youngest child in a family. The origin of so odd a name was probably this. When the birth of a first child is expected, and a basket of child-bed linen is to be provided, the female friends of the expectant mother made contributions to it, principally of their own needlework, as laced caps, cambric robes, silk wrappers, etc. Among them a large pin-cushion is always conspicuously ornamental. It is generally made of white satin, trimmed with silk or silver fringe, with tassels at the

---

* . . . There was a letter to "my dear, dearest Molly," begging her, when she left her room, whatever she did, to go *up* stairs before coming *down*."—Cranford, by Mrs. Gaskell, London. Smith, Elder, and Co., 15, Waterloo Place, 1870, p. 70.

corners. It is always the work of some unmarried lady, to whom it affords an exercise of her taste and ingenuity in disposing pins of different lengths, inserted into the cushion only by their points, in various and fanciful forms, so as to produce some resemblance of a light and elegant basket. These pins are never drawn out for use. The most sensible and experienced nurses would think that a thing of very evil omen. . . . So when the good woman has had a safe getting up it is put aside, and brought forward on the next occasion. On the birth of the last it would seem to fall to him or her as a sort of heirloom. . . .

Forby. "Voc. of E. Anglia," p. 252.

Babies born during "chime hours" have the faculty of seeing spirits and cannot be bewitched. The chime hours are three, six, nine, and twelve,—though an old nurse of the writer's acquaintance stated them as four, eight, and twelve. Children born with a caul are also born to good luck, and can never be drowned. Seamen have great faith in the virtues of a caul, believing that having one about their persons preserves them from all the dangers of the sea. As much as twenty guineas has sometimes been given for this valuable charm.

J. T. Varden. "E. A. Handbook," p. 107.

SUPERSTITIONS ABOUT NEW-BORN CHILDREN.

It is unlucky to weigh them. If you do, they will probably die, and, at any rate, will not thrive. . . .

It is not good for children to sleep upon bones—that is, upon the lap. . . .

Cats suck the breath of infants, and so kill them. . . .

A mother must not go outside her own house-door till she goes to be churched. . . .

If you rock an *empty* cradle, you will rock a new baby into it. . . .

. . . There is a widely-spread notion among the poorer classes, that rice, as an article of food, prevents the increase of the population. . . . It is certain that there was not long ago a great outcry against the giving of rice to poor people under the poor law, as it was said to be done with a purpose.

Suffolk.   C. W. J., "Book of Days," vol. ii, p. 39.

At the birth of a first-born it is the custom that every visitor should give the nurse a present.

It is essential that both child and mother should come downstairs for the first time on a Sunday, and that the mother should go to church on a Sunday, when she first leaves the house.

Everything must be done on Sunday for the first time, in order that it may be successful.

The nurse washes a new-born child with gin to give it a fine complexion.

[From Mr. Redstone, Woodbridge.]

If a baby's finger nails are *cut* before it is a year old it will become a thief, hence they are generally bitten off.

J. T. Varden, "E. A. Handbook," p. 107.

Holy Baptism has also its signs and tokens. . . . If the child cries at the pouring on of the water it is a good sign; if it does not it will die—it is too good for this world.

Ibid. p. 108.

————

IV.—CURE CHARMS.

Many villages in the rural districts of the county are able to boast of their professor of the healing art, in the person of an old woman, who "bless" and "charm" away different maladies, especially wounds from scalding or burning, and who pretend to the power of curing diseases by certain cabalistic signs. . . . Two preliminaries are given as necessary to be strictly observed, in order to ensure a perfect cure. First, that the person to be operated upon comes with a full and earnest belief that a cure will be effected; and secondly, that the phrases "please" and "thank you" do not occur during the transaction. The established formula consists in the charmer's crossing the part affected, and whispering over it certain mysterious words. There is a very prevalent notion that if once disclosed, these mysterious words immediately lose their virtue. . . . In consequence of this secrecy, it is difficult to ascertain what words are employed, the possessors generally being proof against persuasion or bribery. It must not be supposed that these ignorant people make a trade of their supposed art; on the contrary, it is believed that any offer of pecuniary remuneration would at once break the spell, and render the charm of no avail.

A clergyman calling at a cottage one day, saw a small loaf hanging up oddly in a corner of the house. He asked why it was placed there, and was told that it was a *Good Friday loaf*, a loaf baked on Good Friday, that it would never get mouldy, and that it was very serviceable against some diseases, the bloody flux being mentioned as an example. Some weeks after, the clergyman called again with a friend at the same house, and drew his attention to the loaf which was hanging in its accustomed corner. The owner of the house, full of zeal to do the honours of his establishment, endeavoured to take the loaf gently down, but failing in the attempt, he gave a violent pull, and the precious loaf, to his great dismay, was shivered into atoms. The old man collected the fragments and hung them up again in a paper bag, with all the more reverence on account of the good which the loaf, as he alleged, had done his son. The young man, having being seized with a slight attack of English cholera, in the summer, secretly "abscinded" and ate a piece of the loaf, and when his family expressed astonishment at his rapid recovery, he explained the mystery by declaring that he had eaten of the Good Friday loaf and had been cured by it. . . . It was ascertained from other persons that such loaves were far from being uncommon in the parish.

See Forby. "Vocabulary of E. Anglia," vol. ii, p. 402.

Cures for the Whooping Cough.—Procure a live flat-fish—a "little dab" will do; place it whilst alive on the bare chest of the patient, and keep it there till it is dead.

If several children are ill, take some of the hair of the eldest child, cut it into small pieces, and put them into some milk, and give the compound to the youngest child to drink, and so on throughout the family.

Or let the patient eat a roasted mouse; or, let the patient drink some milk which a ferret has lapped; or, let the patient be dragged under a gooseberry bush or bramble, both ends of which are growing in the ground. It is also said that to pass the patient through a slit in the stem of a young ash tree is a certain cure.

Some people procure hair from the cross on the back of a donkey, and having placed it in a bag, hang it round the necks of their invalid children. The presumed efficacy in this hair is connected no doubt with the fact that the ass is the animal which was ridden by JESUS, and with the superstition that the cross was imprinted on its back as a memorial of that event.

An instance is known of a woman who obtained a certain number of "hodmidods" or small snails. These were passed through the hands of the invalids and then suspended in the chimney on a string, in the belief that as they died the whooping cough would leave the children. At Monk's Eleigh a live frog was hung up the chimney, in the belief that its death by such means would effect a cure.

Cures for the Ague.—Miss Strickland, in her "Old Friends and New Acquaintances," thus mentions a superstition that existed in her own district of the county. "Go to the four cross ways to-night, all alone, and just as the clock strikes twelve, turn yourself about three times and drive a tenpenny nail into the ground up to the head, and walk away from the place backwards before the clock is done striking, and you'll miss the ague; but the next person who passes over the nail will take it in your stead."

The Rev. Hugh Pigot, late of Hadleigh, says that during his residence at Hadleigh a few years ago, he, whilst suffering from ague, was strongly urged to go to a stile—one of those that are placed across footpaths—and to drive a nail into that part over which foot passengers travel in their journeys.

Miss Strickland thus speaks of another remedy for this disease. . . . 'In one district of Suffolk I have heard of the following superstitious practice. A man who had been labouring under an obstinate ague for several months purchased a new red earthenware pan in which he put the parings of his fingers and toe nails, together with a lock of hair, and a small piece of raw beef, which in order to render the charm effectual, he considered it necessary to steal. He then tied a piece of black silk over the pan and buried it in the centre of a wood, in ground that had never been broken, in the firm belief that, as the meat decayed, his fever would abate and finally disappear. . . .

To swallow a spider or its web when placed in a small piece of apple is an acknowledged cure for the ague. Miss Strickland heretically mentions an instance of its being tried in vain; but its failure excited great astonishment. "As true as I'm alive, he (the ague) neither minded pepper and gin taken fasting on a Friday morning, nor blackbottle spiders made into pills with fresh butter." The patient should take a handful of salt and bury it in the ground, and as the salt dissolves, the patient will recover from the ague. Or the patient should gather some teasels from the hedgerows, and carry them about his person.

There was formerly a person in Hadleigh who charmed away the ague by pronouncing, or, rather, muttering, over each child a verse of Holy Scripture, taken, it was believed, from the Gospel of St. John.

To Prevent Swelling from a Thorn.—

> "Christ was of a Virgin born,
> And crowned with a crown of thorns;
> He did neither swell nor rebel,
> And I hope this never will."

—At the same time let the middle finger of the right hand keep

in motion round the thorn, and at the end of the words, three
times repeated, touch it every time with the tip of your finger,
and with God's blessing you will find no further trouble.

To Stop Bleeding from Wounds and Arteries Cut or Bruised.—
Repeat these words three times, desiring the blessing of God:

> "Stand fast; lie as Christ did
> When he was crucified upon the cross;
> Blood, remain up in the veins,
> As Christ's did in all his pains!"

To Cure Bleeding at the Nose.—Wear a skein of scarlet silk round
the neck, tied with nine knots down the front. If the patient is
a male, the silk should be put on and the knots tied by a female,
and *vice versa.*

To Cure Toothache.—Always dress and undress the left leg and foot
before the right one. Mr. Rayson, writing in "The East Anglian,"
says that he has known this habit adopted and continued through
life.

The Rev. Hugh Pigot says: "There was an old woman, of
very witch-like appearance, who was supposed to have great skill
in curing burns. She prepared a kind of ointment, and when a
patient applied to her she placed some of it upon the part affected,
then made the sign of the cross over it, and muttered certain
mysterious words, which she would not disclose to any one."
After many enquiries with the view of ascertaining what were
the words employed on these occasions, the reverend gentleman
heard from a man the following curious formula, the words of
which must be repeated three times:—

> "There were three Angels came from the North,
> One brought fire, the other brought frost;
> Come out fire, go in frost,
> Father, Son, and Holy Ghost."

There are many variations of this charm, but in substance the
above is correct.

There are many persons who profess to be able to cure warts, or "writs," as they are called, by passing the hand over them, and muttering at the same time some mysterious word. The operator takes care to ensure his credit against mishaps, for as a necessary condition of success, he must be told the *exact* number of warts which are worn by the applicant for a cure. If, therefore, the remedy fails, he attributes the failure to his having been kept in ignorance of the real number of warts.

If persons have any scruple against consulting such accredited professors of the healing art, they may get rid of their warts in other ways. Thus, let the patient *steal* (it must be stolen, or it will have no efficacy) a piece of beef and bury it in the ground, and then as the beef decays, the warts will gradually die away. Or, go to an ash tree, which has its "keys," that is, husks with seeds upon it, cut the initial letter both of your Christian and surname on the bark, count the exact number of your warts, and cut as many notches in addition to the letters as you have warts, and then as the bark grows up your warts will go away. Or, take the froth of new beer, apply it to your warts when no one sees you (for secrecy is absolutely necessary), do not wipe it away, but let it work off of itself, for three mornings, and your warts will disappear. Or, gather a green sloe, rub it on your warts, then throw it over your *left* shoulder, and you will soon be free from them.

To hang a flint with a hole in it over the head of your bed is a preservative against the nightmare.

Another remedy is, before you go to bed, place your shoes carefully by the bedside "coming and going," that is, with the heel of one pointing in the direction of the toe of the other, and then you will be sure to sleep quietly and well.

To cure, or rather to prevent cramp, take the small bone of a leg of mutton, and carry it always about with you in your pocket. Or, wear a ring made out of an old coffin handle on one of the fingers. The parish clerks have been known to preserve the old coffin handles found in churchyards for the purpose of making *cramp rings*.

To Cure Wens or Fleshy Excrescences.—Pass the hand of a dead body over the part affected, on three successive days. The Rev. Hugh Pigot has known this to be tried at Hadleigh.

> "The New Suffolk Garland," edited by John Glyde, jun., Ipswich.

Mrs. Bunn, a person living at Clopton, used to bless burns. This gift, Mr. Hooke believes, she inherited from her mother. Some years ago Mr. Hooke burnt his hand, and he went to Mrs. Bunn to have it blessed. She moistened her finger with her tongue, and touched the burn, uttering certain words known only to herself. The pain was relieved for about an hour, after which it returned.

> (Told to Camilla Gurdon by the Rev. S. Hooke, Rector of Clopton.)

. . . A galvanic ring, as it is called, worn on the finger, will cure rheumatism. One sometimes sees people with a clumsy-looking silver ring which has a piece of copper let into the inside, and this, though in constant contact throughout, is supposed (aided by the moisture of the hand) to keep up a gentle, but continued galvanic current, and so to alleviate or remove rheumatism.

. . . I recollect that when I was a boy a person came to my father (a clergyman) and asked for a 'sacramental shilling,' *i.e.*, one out of the alms collected at the Holy Communion, to be made into a ring and worn as a cure for epilepsy.

Fright is . . . looked upon as a cure for ague. I suppose that, on the principle that *similia similibus curantur*, it is imagined that the shaking induced by the fright will counteract and destroy the shaking of the ague fit. An old woman has told me that she was actually cured in this manner when she was young. . . .

Fried mice are relied on as a specific for the small-pox, and I am afraid that it is considered necessary that they should be fried *alive*.

With respect to whooping cough, again it is believed that if you ask a person riding on a piebald horse what to do for it, his recommendation will be successful if attended to. My grandfather at one time always used to ride a piebald horse, and he has frequently been stopped by people asking for a cure for whooping cough. His invariable answer was, 'Patience and water-gruel.'

Ear-rings are considered to be a cure for sore eyes; . . . their efficacy is believed in even after the ear has healed.

Warts are expected to be cured by charms. A gentleman well known to me states that, when he was a boy, the landlady of an inn where he happened to be, took compassion on his warty hands, and undertook to cure them by rubbing them with bacon. It was necessary, however, that the bacon should be *stolen*; so the good lady *took it secretly* from her own larder. . . . A near neighbour of mine has the credit of being able to charm warts away by counting them. I have been told by boys that she has actually done so for them, and that the warts have disappeared. . . .

There is a very distressing eruption about the mouth and throat, called the thrush, common among infants and persons in the last extremity of sickness. There is a notion that a person must have it once in his life, either at his birth or death . . . if a sick person shows it, he is given over as past recovery.

Suffolk. C. W. J., Chambers's "Book of Days," vol. i, p. 732.

Typhus Fever.—The milt or spleen of a cow, or the skirt of a sheep, applied to the feet is supposed to "draw" the fever from the head, and thus bring about a speedy cure. Some article of church plate placed upon the patient's stomach is also deemed very efficacious in this and kindred diseases.

J. T. Varden. "E. A. Handbook for 1885," p. 104.

Warts.—Procure a snail ("dodman") and a thorn from a gooseberry bush, pierce the former with the thorn, and anoint the warts with the shrine from it. Then bury the "dodman" without removing the thorn, and as it decays the warts will disappear. Strict secrecy is necessary to the success of this remedy. Count the number of warts exactly, and they will begin at once to waste, and finally go altogether. Bury a *stolen* piece of beef in the ground, as the beef decays the warts will waste away. A

highly approved remedy is also the making of the sign of the
cross on each wart with a pin or pebble, which is afterwards to
be thrown away.

Wens or Moles.—For these excrescences the popular charm is to
pass the hand of a dead* man over them for three days in succession,
the hand of a suicide or executed murderer being deemed more
efficacious than that of one who has died a natural death.

Whooping Cough.—Hold the head of a live frog within the mouth
of the child; then hang up in the chimney till it wastes; or a
number of small "dodmans" are passed through the child's hands
and hung in the same place. As they waste the cough takes
its leave. . . . In some places the child is passed through a split
ash-tree, or dragged three times under a gooseberry-bush or bramble
which has both ends growing in the ground; or it is laid face
downwards on the turf in a meadow, and the turf cut round it
in the shape of a coffin, the child is taken up, and the flag turned
roots uppermost, and as the grass withers the cough wastes. Or
again, a large hole is dug in the meadow, and the child placed
in it in a bent posture and *head downwards*; the turf removed in
making the hole is then placed over him, and so remains until
the poor little sufferer coughs. This must be done in the evening,
and, like the last mentioned, in secrecy. . . .

J. T. Varden, "East Anglian Handbook," p. 105.

Cures for Whooping Cough (Woodbridge).—Lift the patient over
and under the back of a crossed donkey—*i.e.*, a donkey bearing
the sign of the cross.

Let the patient wear a piece of tarred rope as a necklace.

For Rheumatism.—Ashes of a mouse baked alive.

From Mr. Redstone.

---

* Miss M., of Woodbridge, suffering from an affection of the throat, was advised
to lay the hand of a dead person upon her throat in order to effect a cure.

(From Mr. Redstone.)

A Suffolk Cure for Whooping Cough.—I was told of a wonderful cure for whooping cough lately by a woman in the place. Cut a slice of bread, wrap it in a piece of rag, and bury it. When it has been buried three days take it up and eat it. This woman had buried three slices on three different days, and when the last one was buried she took up the first and gave it to her child, sopped in milk with sugar. The bread has an earthy taste, which " does a deal of good."

R. M. S. " Suffolk Notes and Queries." Ipswich Journal, 1877.

Whooping Cough.—The parent of the child finds a dark spider in her *own house*, holds it over the head of the child, and repeats the following :—

" Spider as you waste away,
Whooping-cough no longer stay."

The insect must then be placed in a bag and hung up over the fireplace ; when the spider has wasted away the cough will be gone.

J. T. Varden. " E. A. Handbook for 1885," p. 101.

To Extract a Thorn from the Flesh :—

" Jesus of a maid was born,
He was pinched with nails and thorn,
Neither blains nor boils did fetch at the bone,
No more shall this, by Christ our Lord. Amen.
Lord, bless what I have said, Amen.
So be it unto thee as I have said."

Cure for Cramp.—Cramp bone. The *Patella* of a sheep or lamb. This charm is still in use by some few individuals . . . it is carried in the pocket—the nearer the skin the better, . . . or laid under the pillow at night. I have heard that some of strong nerve . . . have been known so temerarious as to wear the more potent spell of a human *patella*."

Ed. Moor. " Suffolk Words and Phrases," p. 89.

Caul. — The old superstition respecting a child's *caul* is still retained among us. One for sale is occasionally, though but rarely, advertised in our county newspapers. It is supposed to secure good fortune to the wearer, and to be a preservative from drowning.

Ibid. p. 71.

Something like the following conversation passed the other day between a friend of mine and an old Suffolk gamekeeper. My friend had been suffering from rheumatism, and on this day was complaining of being more stiff than usual. "Well, sir," said the old man, " do you carry a potatoe in your pocket?" My friend replied that he had never heard of that as a remedy for rheumatism. "Well, sir, do ye try it. I have carried one in my pocket for many years. Only, mind ye, sir, it must be stolen. You must get it out of a neighbour's field." And upon this the keeper produced out of his pocket an ancient potatoe black with age, dry and hard as a racket ball. "Well Keeper, has it cured your rheumatism?" " I do'ent exactly know, sir, but I haven't had much of it lately."

D. "The East Anglian," new series, vol. iii, p. 371.

The Nightmare.—I recently observed a large stone, having a natural hole through it, suspended inside a Suffolk farmer's cowhouse. Upon inquiry of a labourer, I was informed this was intended as a preventive of nightmare in the cattle. My informant (who evidently placed great faith in its efficacy) added that a similar stone suspended in a bedroom, or a knife or steel laid under the foot of the bed, was of equal service to the sleeper, and that he had frequently made use of this charm.

J. B. C. (Vol. iv, p. 154.) Choice Notes (Folk-Lore from *Notes and Queries*), 1889. The vols. refer to *Notes and Queries.*

All medicine should be taken "next the heart," which means, in the dialect of Suffolk, that the best time for taking medicine is to take it in the morning, fasting.

" The New Suffolk Garland," p. 179.

A lady who has married, but who has not by marriage changed her maiden name, is the best of all persons to administer medicine, since no remedy given by her will ever fail to cure.

"The New Suffolk Garland," p. 179.

There was, and perhaps still is, an idea in Suffolk that an infant will cut its teeth more easily wearing a necklace, ordinary glass beads or seeds strung together being sufficient for the purpose.

R. "Suffolk Notes and Queries," Ipswich Journal, 1877.

Charm against Bleeding at the Nose.—I have, when I was a child, seen women at the village shop buying a skein of scarlet silk to stop bleeding at the nose in children.

A. W. T. "Suffolk Notes and Queries," Ipswich Journal, 1877.

In Woodbridge, Mr. Redstone has seen persons wearing a piece of red velvet round their necks to prevent bleeding at the nose.

Tench.—We have a notion very prevalent that this fish has a healing quality; and that the pike when wounded cures itself by rubbing against the tench, which is not therefore devoured by this, otherwise indiscriminating "fresh water shark."—Nares shows, from Walton and others, that this notion has been widely entertained. . . .

Ed. Moor. "Suffolk Words and Phrases," p. 424.

Sty or Styney.—A troublesome little excrescence or pimple on the eyelid. We fancy that the application of gold, especially of a gold ring, and more especially of a wedding-ring, is a cure. . . .

" — I have a sty here Chilax.
Chi.—I have no gold to cure it ; not a penny."
Beaumont and Fletcher, Mad. Lov., v. 4.
Ibid. p. 408.

*A Snake's Avel.**—Snakes seem pretty nigh exterminated now in Suffolk, but when I wer a boy there wer a few, and the avel

---

* *Avel.*—The beard or *awns* of barley. The corn is said to be *avely*, if, when dressed for market, a portion of the awms adhere to the grains.

Ibid. p. 10.

of a snake—we used not to say 'skin' but snake's avel, we used
—that wer said to be a sure cure for the head-ache, if you wore it
inside of your hat. I wer very subject to the head-ache as a boy,
and I found a snake's avel and wore it in my hat nigh upon a
year, until it dropped to powder, and I lost the head-ache; I
don't know if it wer the snake's avel that did it, or if I out-grew
the head-ache.

(Taken down from the old gardener at Grundisburgh Hall.)

Cure for Epilepsy or Hysteria.—If a young woman has fits she
applies to ten or a dozen unmarried men (if the sufferer be a
man, he applies to as many maidens) and obtains from each of
them a small piece of silver of any kind, as a piece of broken
spoon or ring, or brooch, or buckle, or even sometimes a small
coin, and a penny (without telling the purpose for which the
pieces are wanted); the twelve pieces of silver are taken to a
silversmith, or other worker in metal, who forms therefrom a ring,
which is to be worn by the person afflicted on the fourth finger
of the left hand. If any of the silver remains after the ring is
made, the workman has it as his perquisite, and the twelve pennies
are intended as the wages for his work, and he must charge no more.
" The New Suffolk Garland," p. 170.

In 1830 I went into a gunsmith's shop in the village where
I then resided, and seeing some fragments of silver in a saucer,
I had the curiosity to enquire about them, when I was informed
that they were the remains of the contributions for a ring for the
above purpose, which he had lately been employed to make.
B.   " Choice Notes " (Folk-lore from " Notes and
Queries "), vol. ii, p. 4.

Old Sows (s. pl. millepedes, woodlice).—The species that rolls
itself up on being touched, if swallowed in that state as pills,
are believed to have much medicinal virtue in scrofulous cases,
especially if they be gathered from the roots of aromatic pot
herbs, mint, marjoram, etc.
Forby.   " Vocab. of E. Anglia," vol. ii, p. 238.

Snickup, v. begone ; away with you. . . . When Malvolio comes to disturb the midnight revels of Sir Toby and his drunken companions, the Knight bids him "sneckup!" that is, go and be hanged. A silly sort of childish charm is frequently to be heard, used perhaps by children only, supposed to be very efficacious in curing the hiccup. It is this, "Hickup! *snickup!* rise up, right up! Three sups in a cup are good for the hiccup!" If these potent words (given with some variation in Moor's "Suffolk Words" and Brockett's "Glossary") can be deliberately repeated thrice, and as many sips of cold water taken, without the return of the singultus, the cure is complete.

Forby. *Ibid.* vol. ii, p. 313.

See Ed. Moor in "Suffolk Words and Phrases," p. 167, who gives a slightly different version :—

" Hiccup—sniccup—look up—right up—
Three drops in a cup is good for the hiccup."

Christening a Cure for Sickness.—It is generally believed by East Anglian nurses that a child never thrives well till it is named ; and this is one cause of the earnest desire, frequently expressed, to have children privately baptised. If the child is sick, it is even supposed to promote the cure.

Forby. *Ibid.* vol. ii, p. 406.

The image of S. Petronille demolished " in a chapel near Ipswich " was in the church dedicated to that saint. This church is mentioned in Domesday. . . . It is thought that the church stood in the farm (now reputed extra-parochial) formerly called " Parnels," but for more than a century " Purdis." . . . Pieces of this saint's skull were relics in Bury Abbey, and it was claimed for them that they were cures for all kinds of ague.

Henry C. Casley. " The East Anglian " or " Notes and Queries," new series, vol. ii, p. 68.

The Nail that has Lamed a Horse.—The belief has still some vitality amongst us that the way to recover a horse from the

7 *

lameness caused by puncture of the foot from treading on a nail, is not merely to keep the nail that inflicted the wound, but also to take care that it has been thoroughly cleaned, and is bright, and to see that it is well greased. Some years ago while driving by the old shipyard in Stoke my horse was lamed by this mischance. He had set his foot on a piece of plank from which a nail was protruding. The wound was bad, and the recovery was slow. My coachman, however, had no doubt from the first. He confidently assured me that the recovery was certain, for he had at the time brought away the nail, had carefully cleaned and polished it, and was daily greasing it thoroughly. . . . As late as the year 1884 I met with an instance of the survival of this superstition. A man produced from his pocket, and showed to me the offending nail which he believed would, as long as he kept it bright, aid in the recovery of the lameness it had caused. I forgot to ask him whether he kept it greased.

Bacon notes the same misbelief respecting the sword,* that if the blade, after a wound has been inflicted with it, be kept. anointed with some soothing balm, the healing process will be greatly assisted; but that if contrariwise, the blade be anointed with some poisonous preparation, the wound will thereby be aggravated.

"Some Materials for the Hist. of Wherstead," by
F. B. Zincke, p. 180.

There is no place properer than this where I may mention a custom which I have seen twice practised in this garden within a few years, namely, that of drawing a child through a cleft tree. For this purpose a young ash was each time selected and split longtitudinally about five feet; the fissure was kept wide open by my gardener while the friend of the child, having first stripped him naked, passed him thrice through it, always head foremost.

---

* See Sir Kenelm Digby's "Discourse on the Powder of Sympathy" (1658), wherein he quotes formulae from Paracelsus for application of ointment or blood to a sword or other weapon that made the wound, whereby the wound is healed.

As soon as the operation was performed, the wounded tree was bound up with pack-thread, and as the bark healed the child was to recover. The first of these young patients was to be cured of the rickets; the second of a rupture.

Sir J. Cullum. " Hist. and Antiquities of Hardwick," p. 269.

I have very recently—February, 1834—seen the boy and his parents, who was *draawn* through my young ash at Woodbridge. . . . I often see the boy. He is about eight years old. His mother has assured me that it was a sad case—" so painful, and so *tedious* was the child, that she got no rest night nor day"—and that the child—about six months old when *draawn*—immediately, or very soon, became composed, decidedly mended, and gradually recovered as the tree did; and has ever since remained well. His parents only were present at the operation. I have occasionally called to tell the mother of the well-doing of the tree—evidently to her satisfaction. . . . I have little doubt but I could find out half a score of persons who have been *draawn* in their infancy, and cured, in and about *Woodbridge*. At my last visit to the cured boy, his father, at my request, furnished me with the following memorandum in his own writing:—" In putting a child through a Tree first observe it must be early in the spring before the tree begin to vegitate 2ly the tree must be split as near east and west as it can 3ly it must be done just as the sun is rising 4ly the child must be stript quite naked 5 it must be put through the tree feet foremost 6 it must be turned round with the sun and observe it must be put through the tree 3 times and next you must be careful to close the tree in a proper manner and bind it up close with some new bass or something to answer as well—James Lord was put through and was cured, Mrs Shimming of *Pittistree* had 3 children born " (a word, perhaps *ruptured*, is omitted) " and Mr. Whitbread gave her a tree for each of them and was all cured and there is a man now living in *Woodbridge* who when a child was cured in the same way."

Ed. Moor. "Oriental Fragments," p. 522.

About ten years ago an infant was passed through a split ash in the parish of Woodbridge. The father of the child described the ceremony to Mr. Redstone. It took place on a cold December morning at sunrise, and the naked child was passed through the tree so as to face the rising sun. So great was the parents' belief in the efficacy of the cure that it did not occur to them that there was any danger in exposing the delicate infant to the cold.

Robert C., aged 85, rises at 5.30 a.m., like Mistress Pepys, to *bathe in the 'dag' or dew*, as he "thought it might do his eyes good." He suffers from cataract.

From Mr. Redstone.

Grose tells us that "a slunk or abortive calf, buried in the highway over which cattle frequently pass, will greatly prevent that misfortune happening to cows. This is commonly practised in Suffolk."

Brand's "Pop. Antiquities," vol. iii, p. 167.

St. Etheldred, or St. Audry, Thetford.—This church was seated in the Suffolk part of the borough. . . . "In Thetford . . . there was a parish church, which is now destroyed, called St. Audrise. In this church, among other reliques, was the smock of St. Audrise, which was there kept as a great jewel and precious relique. The virtue of that smock was mighty and manifold, but specially in putting away the toth-ach and the swelling of the throte, so that the paciente were fyrste of all shriven and hard masse, and did such oblations as the priest of the church enjoyned (*Becon's Reliques of Rome, fol.* 181). The vulgar supposed this relique to be so full of sacred virtue, that they ordered in their will certain persons to go in pilgrimage to it for the salvation of their souls. Margaret Whoop, of East Herling, had the following clause in her will, which was dated 1501 : "I will that another man go in pilgrimage for me to Thetford, and offer for me to St. Audry's smock."

"Hist. of Thetford," by T. Martin. London : J.
Nichols, MDCCLXXIX, p. 79.

For Ague.—When a fit is on, the sufferer is to take a short stick and cut in it as many notches as there have been fits, including the present fit; then tie a stone to the stick, throw them privately into a pond, leave it without looking back, and the ague fits will cease. It is indispensable that the strictest secrecy be maintained. This alleged remedy has been communicated to me by two aged persons who place the most unbounded faith in its efficacy.

> Clare. J. B. A., " The E. Anglian," or " Notes and Queries," edited by S. Tymms, vol. iii, p. 130.

To Cure St. Vitus's Dance.—I remember that when I was a boy, a young woman in this place was afflicted with *St. Vitus's Dance*, and to cure her the town band frequently played in her mother's cottage of an evening.

> Clare. John B. Armstead, " E. Anglian," edited by S. Tymms, vol. ii.

V.—DEATH OMENS.

If a corpse is *supple* after death, it is a sign that there will be another death in that family before very long.

> " The New Suffolk Garland," p. 179.

During the interval between death and burial of a body is sometimes spoken of in Suffolk as "lying by the wall." There was formerly a saying "If one lie by the wall on Sunday there will be another (another corpse in the same parish) before the week is out."

> R. Suffolk. " Notes and Queries," Ipswich Journal, 1877.

If a grave is open on Sunday, there will be another dug in the week. . . . A woman coming down from church, and observing an open grave, remarked : " Ah, there will be somebody else wanting a grave before the week is out! "

> Suffolk. C. W. J., " Book of Days," edited by R. Chambers, vol. ii, p. 52.

If every remnant of Christmas decoration is not cleared out of church before Candlemas-day (the Purification, Feb. 2), there will be a death that year in the family occupying the pew where a leaf or berry is left. An old lady (now dead) whom I knew, was so persuaded of the truth of this superstition, that she would not be content to leave the clearing of her pew to the constituted authorities, but used to send her servant on Candlemas-eve to see, that her own seat at any rate was thoroughly freed from danger.

> Suffolk.   C. W. J., "The Book of Days," edited by
> R. Chambers, vol. ii, p. 52.

If you bring yew into the house at Christmas, amongst the other evergreens used to dress it, you will have a death in the family before the end of the year.

If you overturn a loaf of bread in the oven you will have a death in the house.

> Forby.   "Vocabulary of E. Anglia," vol. ii, p. 413.

To break a looking-glass is exceedingly unlucky, and will bring death to yourself or an intimate friend.

> "The New Suffolk Garland," p. 179.

Belief in death tokens is very prevalent; three raps at a bed's head, and the howling of a dog in front of your house during the night, are warnings that the death of some member of the family is at hand.

> *Ibid.* p. 180.

Taking a sprig of blackthorn, when in blossom, into a house is considered to presage death to some members of the family.

> *Ibid.* p. 180.

The screech of an owl flying past [the window of a sick room] signifies the same [death's being near].

> Suffolk.   C. W. J. "Book of Days," vol. ii, p. 53.

Fires and candles also afford presages of death. Coffins flying out of the former, and winding-sheets gathering down from the latter. A winding-sheet is produced from a candle, if, after it has gathered, the strip, which has run down, instead of being absorbed into the general tallow, remains unmelted ; if under these circumstances, it curls over away from the flame, it is a presage of death to the person in whose direction it points. Coffins out of the fire are hollow *oblong* cinders spirted from it, and are a sign of a coming death in the family. I have seen cinders, which have flown out of the fire, picked up and examined to see what they presaged, for coffins are not the only things that are thus produced. If the cinder, instead of being *oblong*, is *oval*, it is a cradle and predicts the advent of a baby ; while, if it is *round*, it is a purse, and means prosperity.

Suffolk. C. W. J. Ibid. vol. ii, p. 53.

The Tide :—

> " Tide flowing is feared, for many a thing,
> Great danger to such as be sick, it doth bring;
> Sea ebb, by long ebbing, some respite doth give,
> And sendeth good comfort to such as shall live."

T. Tusser. " Five Hundred Points," p. xl.

Mr. Barkis goes out with the Tide.—" He's going out with the tide," said Mr. Peggotty to me, behind his hand. My eyes were dim, and so were Mr. Peggotty's, but I repeated in a whisper, ' With the tide ? ' ' People can't die along the coast,' said Mr. Peggotty, ' except when the tide's pretty nigh out. They can't be born. unless it's pretty nigh in—not properly born till flood. He's a going out with the tide. It's ebb at half-arter three, slack water half an hour. If he lives till it turns, he'll hold his own till past the flood, and go out with the next tide.'

Charles Dickens. " The Personal History of David
Copperfield," vol. ii, p. 9.

A failure of the Crop of Ash-keys Portends a Death in the Royal Family.—With what obscure traditionary or legendary tale this foolish notion may be connected, it seems impossible to discover.

Probably, however, there is some such connection. But, be this as it may, the notion is still current amongst us. The failure in question is certainly in some seasons very remarkable, and many an old woman believes that, if she were the fortunate finder of a bunch, and could get introduced to the king, he would give her a great deal of money for it.

Forby. "Vocab. of E. Anglia," vol. ii, p. 406.

Watching in the Church Porch on St. Mark's Night.—The belief on this subject is (or rather was) that the apparitions of those who will die, or have any dangerous sickness in the course of the following year, walk into their parish church at midnight, on the 25th of April. Infants and young children not yet able to walk, are said to roll in on the pavement. Those who are to die remain there, but those who are to recover return, after a longer or shorter time, in proportion to the continuance of their future sickness. Those who wish to witness these appearances are to watch in the church porch on the night in question.

Forby. *Ibid.* vol. ii, p. 407.

Death Omens.—If a swarm of bees alight either on a dead *tree* or dead *bough* of a living tree near the house, or if a bird flies indoors or even taps at the window with its beak, or if the clock "loses a stroke" or refuses to go properly, or if the cuckoo's first note be heard in bed, or if a light be shut up in a room or closet at the time unoccupied . . . there will be a death in the family in a short time. The picking of green bloom or May blossom means death to the head of the family into which it is brought, or if an apple or pear-tree blooms twice in the year, the same catastrophe is brought about. . . . If you see four crows in your path, or a snake enters your room, or if the cuckoo give his note from a dead tree, it means coming death to a relative. . .

J. T. Varden. "E. A. Handbook," p. 117.

VI.—FAIRIES (OR FRAIRIES AND PHARISEES).

. . . "Frairy is given as the Suffolk form of fairy. . . . *Pharisee* is the form with which I am myself familiar. *Pharisees' rings* was the name applied in my childhood to the "sour green ringlets" of Shakespeare's "Tempest," while the star-marked fossils—I forget their scientific title—that occasionally turn up in stone droppings, were known as *Pharisees' loaves.*

Olim Agrestis. "Suffolk Notes and Queries," Ipswich Journal *circa*, May, 1877.

In "A Description of England and Wales" (London, 1769), vol. viii, p. 282, under Southwold, is the following passage:— "On the cliff are two batteries, one of which is a regular fortification, with a good parapet, and six guns that are eighteen pounders. The other has only two guns, which are nine pounders. On this hill, and several others that are near it, are the remains of a camp; and where the ground has not been broken up, there are tokens of circular tents called Fairy-hills, round which they suppose the fairies were wont to dance."

Ibid., Ipswich Journal.

Woolpit is the scene of a remarkable story told by William of Newburgh (Hist. Anglic., Lib. i. c. 27). Near the town, he says, were some very ancient trenches (fossæ) called "Wlfpittes" in English, which gave name to it. Out of these trenches there once came, in harvest time, two children, a boy and girl, whose bodies were of a green colour, and who wore dresses of some unknown stuff. They were caught and taken to the village, where for many months they would eat nothing but beans. They gradually lost their green colour. The boy soon died. The girl survived, and was married to a man of Lynn. At first they could speak no English; but when they were able to do so they said that they belonged to the land of St. Martin, an unknown country, where, as they were watching their father's sheep, they heard a loud noise, like the ringing of the bells of St. Edmund's Monastery. And then all at once they found themselves among the reapers in the harvest field at Woolpit. Their country was a Christian land, and had churches. There was no sun there, only a faint twilight; but beyond a broad river there lay a land of light.

> "Handbook for Essex, Suffolk, Norfolk, and Cambridgeshire," London, John Murray, 8vo., 1875, p. 175. (Also given in Keightley's "Fairy Mythology, p. 281.")

I have great pleasure in sending you the "legend" on which I founded the story of "Brother Mike." I believe that my rendering of the dialect is perfectly correct, and may be depended upon, at least for the district round Bury St. Edmunds.

"There wus a farmer, right a long time ago, that wus, an he had a lot o' wate, a good tidy lot o' wate he had. An he huld all his wate in a barn, of a hape he did! but that hape that got lesser and lesser, an he kount sar how that kum no how. But at last he thout he'd go and see if he kount see suffun. So off of his bed he got, one moanlight night, an he hid hiself hind the oud lanetew, where he could see that's barn's doors; an when the clock struck twelve, if he dint see right a lot of little tiddy frairies. O lork! how they did run—they was little bits o' things, as big as mice, an they had little blue caoots and yaller breeches an little red caps on thar hids with long tassels hangin down behind. An they run right up to that barn's door. An if that door dint open right wide of that self. An lopperty lop! over the throssold they all hulled themselves. Well, when the farmer see they wus all in, he kum nigher an nigher, an he looked inter the barn he did. An he see all they little frairies; they danced round an round, an then they all ketched up an air o' wate, an kopt it over their little shouders, they did. But at the last there come right a dear little frairie that wus soo small

that could hardly lift that air o' wate, and that kep saying as
that walked—

> " Oh, how I du twait,
> A carrying o' this air o' wate."

An when that kum to the throssold, that kount git over no how,
an that farmer he retched out his hand an he caught a houd o'
that poooare thing, an that shruck out, ' Brother Mike! Brother
Mike!' as loud as that could. But the farmer he kopt that
inter his hat, an he took that home for his children; he tied
that to the kitchen winder. But that poooare little thing, that
wont ate nothin, an that poyned away and died.

> Cambridge. " Brother Mike." " Suffolk Notes and
> Queries," Ipswich Journal, 1877.

A belief in the existence of " Pharisees" or " Fairies," prevails:
they ride young horses about in the night, so that the grooms
on going into the stables in the morning find the horses all in a
foam. But a hag stone, with a hole through, tied to the key
of the stable door, protects the horses.

> " The New Suffolk Garland," p. 179.

Fairy-Butter, s. a species of *tremella*, of yellowish colour and
gelatinous substance, not very rarely found on furze and broom.
Brockett's Glossary describes it as growing about the roots of old
trees. This must be some other species; probably what is called
in some places witch's-butter; of coarser texture and colour, and
by no means so suitable to those delicate beings the fairies, as that
which we name after them.

Fairy-Rings, s. circles or parts of circles in the grass (due to
a kind of fungus); . . . in which, as many believed of old, and
some believe still, the fairies are wont to dance.

> Forby. " Vocab. of E. Anglia," vol. i, p. 108.

Mermaids are supposed to abound in the ponds and ditches in
this neighbourhood. Careful mothers use them as bugbears to
prevent little children from going too near the water. I once
asked a child what mermaids were, and he was ready with his

answer at once, 'Them nasty things what crome you (i.e. hook you) into the water!' Another child has told me 'I see one wunst, that was a grit big thing loike a feesh.' . . .

> Suffolk.　C. W. J., "The Book of Days," vol. i, p. 678.

When I was quite a child, in 1814, we used to play in a field at Bendlesham where there was a pond at one end with trees round it, the grass in early spring full of flowers. It was always called the S pond, being shaped like an S, so drawn. If we went too near our nursemaid would call out to us not to go so near "lest the mermaid should come and *crome* us in." Crome (crumm) as all East Anglians know, is the same as "crooked"; whence a "*crome* fork" for unloading muck.

> Senex.　" Suffolk Notes and Queries," Ipswich Journal (1877 ?).

Suffolk Superstition.—A well in the village was said to contain a mermaid.—*A. W. T.*

> *Ibid.*, Ipswich Journal (1877 ?).

Perry-Dancers, s. pl. the Northern lights. The *peries* or *perries* are the fairies. There is fancy and elegance in this word. It is corrupted, it seems in Lowland Scotch to *merry-dancers* or *pretty-dancers.*

> Forby.　" Vocabulary of E. Anglia," vol. ii, p. 249.

Stowmarket Fairies. (Feriers or Ferishers.)—The whole of the Hundred is remarkable for fairy stories, ghost adventures, and other marvellous legends.

Fairies frequented several houses in Tavern Street about 80 to 100 years since. They never appeared as long as any one was about. People used to lie hid to see them, and some have seen them. Once in particular by a wood-stack up near the brick-yard there was a large company of them dancing, singing, and playing music together. They were very small people, quite little creatures and very merry. But as soon as they saw anybody they all vanished away. In the houses after they had fled, on going upstairs sparks of fire as bright as stars used to appear under the feet of the persons who disturbed them.

Old Parish Clerk.—Neighbour S—— is a brother of old B—— the sexton. He died·at 82—she is now near 80. Her father was a leather breeches maker, and her mother having had a baby (either herself or her sister she forgets which), was lying asleep some weeks after her confinement in bed with her husband and the infant by her side. She woke in the night, it was dimmish light, and missed the babe. Uttering an exclamation of fear, lest the fairies (or feriers) should have taken the child, she jumped out of bed, and there sure enough a number of the little sandy things had got the baby at the foot of the bed and were undressing it. They fled away through a hole in the floor, laughing as if they shrieked, and, snatching up her child, on examination she found that they had laid all the pins head to head as they took them out of the dress. For months afterwards she always slept with the child between herself and husband, and used carefully to pin it by its bed clothes to the pillow and sheets that it might not be snatched hastily away. This happened in the old house which stood where the new one now stands on the south side of the Vicarage gate.

A woman, as she heard tell, had a child changed, and one, a poor thing, left in his place, but she was very kind to it, and every morning on getting up she found a small piece of money in her pocket. My informant firmly believes in their existence, and wonders how it is that of late years no such things have been seen.

Onehouse.—A man was ploughing in a field, a fairy quite small and sandy-coloured came to him and asked him to mend his peel (a flat iron with a handle to take bread out of an oven) and that if he did he should have a hot cake. The ploughman soon put a new handle in it, and soon after a smoking hot cake made its appearance in the furrows near him, which he ate with infinite relish.

A fairy man came to a woman in the parish and asked her to

attend his wife at her lying-in, she did so and went to fairyland
and afterwards came home none the worse for her trip. But one
Thursday at the market in Stowe, she saw the fairy man in a
butcher's shop helping himself to some beef. On this she goes
up and spoke to him. Whereupon much surprised, he bids her
say nothing about it, and enquires with which eye she could see
him, as in fairy land he had rubbed one of her eyes with some
ointment. On pointing to the gifted eye he blew into it, and
from that time she could never see a fairy again.

The house in which A. W—— now lives was the scene of fairy
visits and officiousness. A man lived there about 100 years since,
who was visited constantly by a fairy (or ferrier or ferisher). They
used his cottage for their meetings. They cannot abide dirt or
slovenliness, so it was kept tidy and clean. They cut and brought
faggots for the good man, and filled his oven with nice dry wood
every night. They also left a shilling for him under the leg of
a chair. And a fairy often came to him and warned him not to
tell any one of it, for if he did the shilling, wood, and fairies
would never come to him again. Unluckily for him he did tell
his good luck, and then his little friends were never seen by him
more. The fairy wore yellow satin shoes, was clothed with a
green long coat, girt about by a golden belt, and had sandy hair
and complexion.

Stowmarket, 1842.—S—— living for 30 years at the cottages
in the hop-ground on the Bury road, coming home one night 20
years since, in the meadow now a hop ground, not far from three
ashen trees, in very bright moonlight, saw the fairies. There
might be a dozen of them, the biggest about three feet high, and
small ones like dolls. Their dresses sparkled as if with spangles,
like the girls at shows at Stow fair. They were moving round
hand in hand in a ring, no noise came from them. They seemed
light and shadowy, not like solid bodies. I passed on saying, the
Lord have mercy on me, but them must be the fairies, and being
alone then on the path over the field could see them as plain as
I do you. I looked after them when I got over the style, and
they were there, just the same moving round and round. I ran

home and called three women to come back with me and see
them. But when we got to the place they were all gone. I
could not make out any particular things about their faces. I
might be forty yards from them and I did not like to stop and
stare at them. I was quite sober at the time.

Hollingworth's "Hist. of Stowmarket," p. 248.

. . . A gentleman-farmer, in the neighbourhood of Woodbridge,
had a calf to sell, and happened to be by when his bailiff and a
butcher were about to bargain for it. The calf was produced,
and was apparently very hot : " Oh ! " said the butcher, " the
Pharisees have been here ; and 'stru's you are alive, have been
riding that there poor calf all night." . . . The butcher very
gravely instructed my friend how to avert such consequences in
future : which was, to get a stone with a hole in it, and hang it
up in the calves' crib," just high enough not to touch the calves'
backs when standing up : " for," added the compassionate man
of knife and steel," it will brush the *Pharisees* off the poor beasts
when they attempt to gallop 'em round." This was a master-
butcher, a shrewd intelligent man, in 1832. It accounted to me
for the suspension of a stone, weighing perhaps a pound, which
I had many years observed in my farm stable, just higher than
the horses' backs. And although my men more than half deny it,
I can discern that they have heard of the Pharisaic freaks, and
more than half believe in them.

Ed. Moor. "Oriental Fragments," p. 456.

Calling at a cottage in a retired lane in the parish of Carlton
Colville, near this town, a few weeks since, I saw on the chimney-
piece what appeared to be a fine specimen of fossil echinus, though
sadly disfigured by the successive coats of black lead used to give
it a polish. . . . I was informed that it had been found on the
land some twenty years before; that it was "a fairy loaf"; and
that whoever had one of these loaves in the house would never
want for bread.

Lowestoft. E., "The East Anglian," or "Notes
and Queries," edited by S. Tymms, vol. iii, p. 45.

VII.—FOLK TALES.

THE SUFFOLK "KING LEAR." CAP O' RUSHES.

(Told by an old servant to the writer when a child.)

Well, there was once a very rich gentleman, and he'd three darters. And he thought to see how fond they was of him. So he says to the first, "How much do you love me, my dear?" "Why," says she, "as I love my life." "That's good," says he.

So he says to the second, "How much do you love me, my dear?" "Why, says she, "better nor all the world." "That's good," says he.

So he says to the third, "How much do *you* love me, my dear?" "Why," she says, "I love you as fresh meat loves salt," says she. Well, he were that angry. "You don't love me at all," says he, "and in my house you stay no more." So he drove her out there and then, and shut the door in her face.

Well, she went away, on and on, till she came to a fen. And there she gathered a lot of rushes, and made them into a cloak, kind o', with a hood, to cover her from head to foot, and to hide her fine clothes. And then she went on and on till she came to a great house.

"Do you want a maid?" says she.

"No, we don't," says they.

"I hain't nowhere to go," says she, "and I'd ask no wages, and do any sort o' work," says she.

"Well," says they, "if you like to wash the pots and scrape the saucepans, you may stay," says they.

So she stayed there, and washed the pots and scraped the saucepans, and did all the dirty work. And because she gave no name, they called her Cap o' Rushes.

Well, one day there was to be a great dance a little way off, and the servants was let go and look at the grand people. Cap o' Rushes said she was too tired to go, so she stayed at home.

But when they was gone, she offed with her cap o' rushes and cleaned herself, and went to the dance. And no one there was so finely dressed as her.

Well, who should be there but her master's son, and what should he do but fall in love with her the minute he set eyes on her. He wouldn't dance with anyone else.

But before the dance were done, Cap o' Rushes she stepped off and away she went home. And when the other maids was back she was framin' to be asleep with her cap o' rushes on.

Well, next morning, they says to her:

"You did miss a sight, Cap o' Rushes!"

"What was that?" says she.

"Why the beautifullest lady you ever see, dressed right gay and ga'. The young master, he never took his eyes off of her."

"Well I should ha' liked to have seen her," says Cap o' Rushes.

"Well, there's to be another dance this evening, and perhaps she'll be there."

But, come the evening, Cap o' Rushes said she was too tired to go with them. Howsumdever, when they was gone, she offed with her cap o' rushes, and cleaned herself, and away she went to the dance.

The Master's son had been reckoning on seeing her, and he danced with no one else, and never took his eyes off of her.

But before the dance was over, she slipped off and home she went, and when the maids came back, she framed to be asleep with her cap o' rushes on.

Next day they says to her again:

"Well, Cap o' Rushes, you should ha' been there to see the lady. There she was again, gay an ga', and the young master he never took his eyes off of her."

"Well, there," says she, "I should ha' liked to ha' seen her."

"Well," says they, "there's a dance again this evening, and you must go with us, for she's sure to be there."

"Well, come the evening, Cap o' Rushes said she was too tired to go, and do what they would she stayed at home. But when they was gone, she offed with her cap o' rushes, and cleaned herself, and away she went to the dance.

The masters's son was rarely glad when he saw her. He danced with none but her, and never took his eyes off her. When she wouldn't tell him her name, nor where she came from, he gave her a ring, and told her if he didn't see her again he should die.

Well, afore the dance was over, off she slipped, and home she went, and when the maids came home she was framing to be asleep with her cap o' rushes on.

Well, next day they says to her: "There, Cap o' Rushes, you didn't come last night, and now you wont see the lady, for there's no more dances."

"Well, I should ha' rarely liked to ha' seen her," says she.

The master's son he tried every way to find out where the lady was gone, but go where he might, and ask whom he might, he never heard nothing about her. And he got worse and worse for the love of her till he had to keep his bed.

"Make some gruel for the young master," they says to the cook, "He's dying for love of the lady." The cook she set about making it, when Cap o' Rushes came in.

"What are you a' doin' on," says she.

"I'm going to make some gruel for the young master," says the cook, "for he's dying for love of the lady."

"Let me make it," says Cap o' Rushes.

Well, the cook wouldn't at first, but at last she said yes; and Cap o' Rushes made the gruel. And when she had made it, she slipped the ring into it on the sly, before the cook took it upstairs.

The young man, he drank it, and saw the ring at the bottom.

"Send for the cook," says he. So up she comes.

"Who made this here gruel?" says he.

"I did," says the cook, for she were frightened, and he looked at her.

"No you didn't," says he. "Say who did it, and you shan't be harmed."

"Well, then, 'twas Cap o' Rushes," says she.

"Send Cap o' Rushes here," says he.

So Cap o' Rushes came.

"Did you make the gruel?" says he.

"Yes, I did," says she.

"Where did you get this ring?" says he.

"From him as gave it me," says she.

"Who are you then?" says the young man.

"I'll show you," says she. And she offed with her cap o' rushes, and there she was in her beautiful clothes.

Well, the master's son he got well very soon, and they was to be married in à little time. It was to be a very grand wedding, and every one was asked, far and near. And Cap o' Rushes' father was asked. But she never told nobody who she was.

But afore the wedding she went to the cook, and says she, "I want you to dress every dish without a mite o' salt."

"That will be rarely nasty," says the cook.

"That don't signify," says she. "Very well," says the cook.

Well, the wedding day came, and they was married. And after they was married, all the company sat down to their vittles.

When they began to eat the meat, that was so tasteless they couldn't eat it. But Cap o' Rushes' father, he tried first one dish and then another, and then he burst out crying.

"What's the matter?" said the master's son to him.

"Oh!" says he, "I had a daughter. And I asked her how much she loved me. And she said, 'As much as fresh meat loves salt.' And I turned her from my door for I thought she didn't love me. And now I see she loved me best of all. And she may be dead for aught I know."

"No, father, here she is," says Cap o' Rushes.

And she goes up to him and puts her arms round him. And so they was happy ever after.

A. W. T. "Suffolk Notes and Queries," Ipswich Journal, 1877.

Tom Tit Tot.

(Told by an old servant to the writer when a child.)

Well, once upon a time there were a woman, and she baked five pies. And when they come out of the oven they was that overbaked, the crust were too hard to eat.   So she says to her darter :

"Maw'r," says she, "put you them there pies on the shelf an' leave 'em there a little, an' they'll come agin."—She meant you know, the crust 'ud get soft.

But the gal, she says to herself, "Well, if they'll come agin, I'll ate 'em now." And she set to work an' ate 'em all, first and last.

Well, come supper time the woman she said : "Goo you and git one o' them there pies. I dare say they've come agin now,"

The gal she went an' she looked, and there warn't nothin' but the dishes. So back she come, and says she, "Noo, they ain't come agin."

"Not none on 'em?" says the mother.

"Not none on 'em," says she.

"Well, come agin, or not come agin," says the woman, "I'll ha' one for supper."

"But you can't, if they ain't come," says the gal.

"But I can," says she, "Goo you an' bring the best of 'em."

"Best or worst," says the gal, "I've ate 'em all, an' you can't ha' one till that's come agin."

Well, the woman she were wholly bate, an' she took her spinnin' to the door to spin, and as she spun she sang :

> " My darter ha' ate five, five pies to-day.
> My darter ha' ate five, five pies to-day."

The King, he were a' comin' down the street an' he hard her sing, but what she sang he couldn't hare, so he stopped and said :

"What were that you was a singin' of, maw'r ? "

The woman, she were ashamed to let him hare what her darter had been a doin', so she sang, 'stids o' that :

> " My darter ha' spun five, five skeins to-day.
> My darter ha' spun five, five skeins to-day."

"S'ars o' mine !" said the king, "I never heerd tell of anyone as could do that."

Then he said : "Look you here, I want a wife and I'll marry your darter. But look you here," says he, "'leven months out o' the year she shall have all the vittles she likes to eat, and all the gownds she likes to git, and all the cump'ny she likes to hev; but the last month o' the year she'll ha' to spin five skeins ev'ry day, an' if she doon't, I shall kill her."

"All right," says the woman, for she thowt what a grand marriage that was. And as for them five skeins, when te come tew, there'd be plenty o' ways o' gettin' out of it, an' likeliest, he'd ha' forgot about it.

Well, so they was married. An' for 'leven months the gal had all the vittles she liked to ate, and all the gownds she liked to git, an' all the cump'ny she liked to hev.

But when the time was gettin' oover, she began to think about them there skeins an' to wonder if he had 'em in mind. But not one word did he say about 'em, an' she whoolly thowt he'd forgot 'em.

Howsivir, the last day o' the last month, he takes her to a room she'd nivir set eyes on afore. There worn't nothin' in it but a spinnin' wheel and a stool. An' says he, "Now me dear, hare yow'll be shut in tomorrow with some vittles and some flax, and if you hain't spun five skeins by the night, yar hid'll goo off."

An' awa' he went about his business. Well, she were that frightened. She'd allus been such a gatless mawther, that she didn't so much as know how to spin, an' what were she to dew to-morrer, with no one to come nigh her to help her. She sat down on a stool in the kitchen, an' lork! how she did cry!

Howsiver, all on a sudden she hard a sort of a knockin' low down on the door. She upped and oped it, an' what should she see but a small little black thing with a long tail. That looked up at her right kewrious, an' that said :

"What are yew a cryin' for ?"

"Wha's that to yew ?" says she.

"Nivir yew mind" that said. "But tell me what you're a cryin' for ?"

"That oon't dew me noo good if I dew," says she.

"You doon't know that," that said, an' twirled that's tail round.

"Well," says she, "that oon't dew no harm, if that doon't dew no good," and she upped and told about the pies an' the skeins an' everything.

"This is what I'll do," says the little black thing. "I'll come to yar winder iv'ry mornin' an' take the flax an' bring it spun at night."

"What's your pay?" says she.

That looked out o' the corners o' that's eyes an' that said: "I'll give you three guesses every night to guess my name, an' if you hain't guessed it afore the month's up, yew shall be mine."

Well, she thowt she'd be sure to guess that's name afore the month was up. "All right," says she, "I agree."

"All right," that says, an' lork! how that twirled that's tail.

Well, the next day, har husband he took her inter the room, an' there was the flax an' the day's vittles.

"Now there's the flax," says he, "an if that ain't spun up this night off goo yar head." An' then he went out an' locked the door.

He'd hardly goon, when there was a knockin' agin the winder.

She upped and she oped it, and there sure enough was the little oo'd thing a settin' on the ledge.

"Where's the flax?" says he.

"Here te be," says she. And she gonned it to him.

Well, come the evenin', a knockin' come agin to the winder. She upped an' she oped it and there were the little oo'd thing, with five skeins of flax on his arm.

"Here te be," says he, an' he gonned it to her.

"Now what's my name?" says he.

"What, is that Bill?" says she.

"Noo, that ain't," says he. An' he twirled his tail.

"Well, is that Ned?" says she.

"Noo that ain't," says he. An' he twirled his tail.

"Well, is that Mark?" says she.

"Noo that ain't," says he. An' he twirled harder, an' awa' he flew.

Well, when har husband he come him, there was the five skeins

riddy for him. "I see I shorn't hev for to kill yow to-night, me
dare," says he. "Yew'll hev yar vittles and yar flax in the
mornin," says he, an' awa' he goes.

Well, ivery day the flax an' the vittles, they was brought, an'
ivery day that there little black impet used for to come mornins'
and evenins'. An' all the day the mawther she set a tryin' fur
to think of names to say to it when te come at night. But she
niver hot on the right one. An' as that got to-warts the ind
o' the month, the impet that began for to look soo maliceful, an'
that twirled that's tail faster and faster each time she gave a guess.

At last te come to the last day but one.

The impet that come at night along o' the five skeins, an' that
said :

"What, hain't yew got my name yet?"

"Is that Nicodemus?" says she.

"Noo t'ain't," that says.

"Is that Sammle?" says she.

"Noo t'ain't," that says.

"A-well, is that Methusalem?" says she.

"Noo t'ain't that norther," he says.

Then that looks at her with that's eyes like a cool o' fire, an'
that says. "Woman, there's only tomorrer night, an' then yar'll
be mine!" An' awa' te flew.

Well, she felt that horrud. Howsomediver, she hard the King
a comin' along the passage. In he came, an' when he see the
five skeins, he says, says he :

"Well my dare," says he. "I don't see but what you'll ha'
your skeins ready tomorrer night as well, an' as I reckon I
shorn't ha' to kill you, I'll ha' supper in here tonight." So they
brought supper, an' another stool for him, and down the tew
they sat.

Well, he hadn't eat but a mouthful or so, when he stops an'
begins to laugh.

"What is it?" says she.

"A-why," says he, "I was out a huntin' to-day, an' I got
awa' to a place in the wood I'd never seen afore. An' there

was an old chalk pit. An' I heerd a sort of a hummin', kind o'.
So I got off my hobby, an' I went right quiet to the pit, an' I
looked down. Well, what should there be but the funniest little
black thing yew iver set eyes on. An' what was that dewin' on,
but that had a little spinnin' wheel, an' that were spinnin'
wonnerful fast, an' a twirlin' that's tail. An' as that span that
sang .

> " Nimmy nimmy not,
> My name's Tom Tit Tot."

Well, when the mawther heerd this, she fared as if she could
ha' jumped outer her skin for joy, but she di'n't say a word.

Next day, that there little thing looked soo maliceful when he
come. for the flax. An' when night came, she heerd that a
knockin' agin the winder panes. She oped the winder, an' that
come right in on the ledge. That were grinnin' from are to are,
an' Oo! tha's tail were twirlin' round so fast.

"What's my name?" that says, as that gonned her the skeins.

"Is that Solomon?" she says, pretendin' to be afeard.

"Noo t'ain't," that says, an' that come fudder inter the room.

"Well, is that Zebedee?" says she agin.

"Noo t'ain't," says the impet. An' then that laughed an'
twirled that's tail till yew cou'n't hardly see it.

"Take time, woman," that says; "next guess an' you're mine."
An' that stretched out that's black hands at her.

Well, she backed a step or two, an she looked at it, an then
she laughed out, an' says she, a pointin' of her finger at it,

> " Nimmy nimmy not,
> Yar name's Tom Tit Tot."

Well, when that hard her, that shruck awful, an' awa' that
flew into the dark, an' she niver saw it noo more.

A. W. T.   " Suffolk Notes and Queries," Ipswich
Journal, 15 January, 1878.

VIII.—FUNERAL CUSTOMS.

Burial within, or without, the Sanctuary.—To be buried out of the sanctuary does not mean interment in unconsecrated ground, but in some remote part of the church-yard,* apart from that in which the bodies of the inhabitants in general are deposited. In many church-yards may be seen a row of graves on the extreme verge, which are occupied by the bodies of strangers buried at the parish charge, of suicides, or of others, who are considered unfit to associate underground with the good people of the parish. These are said to "lie out of the Sanctuary."

Forby. "Vocabulary of East Anglia," vol. ii, p. 407.

There is a great partiality to burying on the South and East sides of the church-yard. About twenty years ago, when I first became rector, and observed how those sides (particularly the South) were crowded with graves, I prevailed upon a few persons to bury their friends on the North, which was entirely vacant; but the example was not followed as I hoped it would be; and they continue to bury on the South, where a corpse is rarely interred without disturbing the bones of its ancestors.

This partiality may perhaps at first have arisen from the ancient custom of praying for the dead; for as the usual approach to this and most country churches is by the South, it was natural for burials to be on that side, that those who were going to divine service might, in this way, by the sight of the graves of their friends, be put in mind to offer up a prayer for the welfare of their souls. . . . That this motive has its influences, may be concluded from the graves that appear on the North side of the church-yard where the approach to the church happens to be that

---

* See Sir L. Clifford's will (17 Sept., 1404), in which as a penance he orders "his wretchid careyn to be beryed in the ferthest corner of the chirche-zerd." ("Book of Days," vol. ii, p. 350.)

way: of this there are some few instances in this neighbourhood. Still, however, even in this case, the South side is well tenanted; there must therefore have been some other cause of this preference.

In this church-yard stood formerly a *Cross*. . . . Another stood where the direction-post now stands, close to the church-yard and gave the name of Cock's-Crouch* Lane (as appears by old deeds) to the lane at the East end of the Church House.

Crosses were very early erected in church-yards to put passengers in mind to pray for the souls of those whose bodies lay there interred.

"History and Antiquities of Hawsted," by the Rev. Sir J. Cullum, p. 40.

Hawsted Church.—A tablet over the north door has an appropriate epitaph to the historian of the parish, whose remains lie under the great stone at this door in the church-yard. They were interred here according to the direction of his will; a direction given doubtless, as Mr. Gage Rokewode suggests, to mark his contempt, as expressed in the history, for the vulgar superstition of refusing to bury on the north side of the church.

Samuel Tymms. Proceedings of Suffolk Institute of Archæology, vol. ii. Lowestoft: printed by S. Tymms, 60, High Street, MDCCCLIX.

Mr. Redstone knew a girl (Mary C., of Sutton) who when she was dying of consumption, about six years ago, desired her parents to bury her in a certain quiet spot in the north end of the church-yard. The parents objected, and it was only when the girl threatened to haunt them that they gave way. This end of the church-yard (as it appears in ancient records of Woodbridge) was

---

* Cock's Crouch is God's Cross. The first word is corrupted in that manner more than once in Chaucer.

used as a mart, and pigs were sold here to avoid paying the market
dues; the money for them was received in the North Porch.

From Mr. Redstone.

'*Month's Mind*.'—Will of Robert Marshe of Bromswell: In the
name of god amen The Xth day of December in the yer of our
lord god mlccccxxvj I Robert Marshe of Bromyswall in the dioce
of Norwic beyng in good mynd make this my Testment. . . . Itm
I bequeethe for a trentalle to be sang for me in Bromyswall Chyrche
forseid xs. Itm I bequeethe for messys to be song at Scala celi
vs. . . . Itm I wyll haue an honest monthe day kept in Bromyswall
Chyrche forseid w^t mete ℓ drynke as ℓalbe (shall be) thought
sufficient by myñ execut. . . .

Cecil Deedes. "The East Anglian," or "Notes and
Queries," new series, voL ii, p. 233.

Month's mind, s. an eager wish or longing. A very ancient
phrase, many centuries old, in very general use in a different
sense; perhaps now equally general in this. It was a feast in
memory of the dead, held by surviving friends at the end of a
month from the decease.

"The Vocabulary of East Anglia," by Rev. R.
Forby, vol. ii, p. 218.

[Items from the account of the Chaplain of Cecilia Talmache,
deceased in 1281. The chaplain appears to have been the acting
executor.]

Wax, that is wax-candles, bought for the executors and their
servants against the feast of the Purification of the Lady Mary,
vij$d$. This festival was on the 2nd of February, and celebrated
with abundance of candles, both in churches and processions. . . .
On this day were consecrated all the tapers and candles which
were to be used in the church during the year. Hence the
name Candlemas-day.

. . . One mass celebrated for the soul of the Lady and a ringing

for her soul at Hawsted iij*d*. The same at Bury iij*d*. The ringing
of bells was no inconsiderable part of the ceremony at ancient
funerals. . . .

. . . A pair of shoes to a priest for assisting Gilbert the chaplain
in celebrating mass for the lady's soul ij*d*. A pair of shoes as
well as of gloves, seems to have been a common present of old.

> "History and Antiquities of Hawsted," by Sir J.
> Cullum, p. 11.

BELL-MEN.

[Concerning "the will of John Baret, of Bury S. Edmund's,
who died in 1463, and is buried in S. Mary's Church in that
town."]

His directions are most ample. The two bellmen that went
about the town at his death were to have gowns, and to be two
of the five torch-holders, for which they were to have twopence
and their meat, the Sexton receiving twelve pence and his bread,
drink, and meat. At the "yeerday," the bellmen were to receive
fourpence each for going about the town to call on the inhabitants
to pray "for my soule and for my faderis and modrys."

The "Thirty day" (which may spring from the thirty days
mourning for Moses and Aaron) is well known for its Trental
of masses, always of course thirty in number, but varying in
detail from time to time.

. . . We find bellmen employed on the "Thirty day," which
is equivalent to another well-known expression, the "Month's
mind." All the good people of Bury, however, were not of the
same opinion as John Baret. John Coote, for instance, "will
neyther ryngyn nor belman goynge," but his almsgivings and
dinners on his Thirty-day to be "don in secret manner."

Joan Mason, widow of Bury, in 1510, directed the bellmen to
go abowte the parysshe" at her anniversary and earth-tide to
"pray and reherse the sowles" of all the persons she recited.

Another remarkable custom was the sounding by means of a
chime-barrel the *Requiem Eternam*, which as may be seen, ranged

only over five notes. John Baret . . . makes special arrangement for this music during his Thirty-day.

J. Raven. " Church Bells of Suffolk," p. 86.

At Bury the Curfew bell saved the life of John Perfay, draper,
who was not forgetful of the incident, as appears in his will,
dated 1509. " I wole that my close which ys holdyn by copy
off my lord Abbot of Bury Seynt Edmond. . . . I gyve toward
ye ryngers charge off the gret belle in Seynt Mary Churche, callyd
corfew belle."

The original of this bequest is thus related by Mr. Gage Rokewode
(" Hist. of Hengrave,". p. 11). "John Perfey, tenant of the Manor
of Fornham All Saints, is said to have lost his way in returning
from the Court to Bury, and to have recovered himself from a
perilous situation by accident, by hearing the striking of the
clock or *bell* at S. Mary's, Bury. This circumstance, if we are
to believe a tale not uncommon, led to his devising certain pieces
of land, which took the name of Bell meadow, parcel of the manor
of Fornham All Saints, to the Churchwardens of S. Mary's, in order
that the bell might be tolled in summer regularly at four o'clock
in the morning and nine in the evening, and in winter at six in
the morning and eight at night."

Mr. Gage Rokewood is very likely right in thinking that one
purpose of this endowment was to incite the people to repeat the
Angelus.

Ibid. p. 88.

[From a book of account, intitled, "Coosts laid out at the
monthes mynde, 1540," of Sir Thomas Kytson, buried at Hengrave.]

Paide and laid out by t'hands of Mr. John Crofts, Esqueyr, for
coosts and chardge and in meat and drynke, ware for the heresse
and making of hit, and for the setting of it up, and in dole with
other chardge and necessarys done at the monthes mynde at Hengrave. . . . xxxv*li.* xviij*s.* vj*d.*

"Gage's Hengrave," p. 113.

[From the inventory of the effects of the deceased.] Wares in the warehouses in London, i^m. i^c. iiij^xxj*li*. xv*s*. j*d*.

[These consisted of cloth of gold, sattins, tapistry, velvets, furs, fustians, bags of pepper, cloves, madder, etc. Among the wares appears a curious item : Itm, a hundryth wyght of amuletts for the neke, xxc. xvj*ll*, iiij*s*, j*d*.]

Dr. Hering in his " Preservatives againts the Pestilence," 4to London, 1625, has the following passage : " Perceiving many in this citie to weare about their necks upon the region of the heart certain placents or amulets (as preservatives against the pestilence) confected of arsenick, my opinion is, that they are so farre from effecting any good in tis kind, as a preventive, that they are very dangerous and hurtful if not pernitious to those that weare them."

" Gage's Hengrave," p. 115.

Sir Thomas de Hemegrave died on the seventeenth of October, 1419. . . . He bequeathed . . to each of the poor, called bed lawer-men, within the said city (Norwich) fourpence, to pray for his soul. " Laying out the corpse," says Brand, is an office always performed by women, who claim the linen, etc., about the person of the deceased at the time of performing the ceremony, etc.— *Popular Antiquities.* Yet this was the office of these bedlayer men, and it is a duty performed by the brethren of the Misericordia.

Ibid. p. 91.

WOODBRIDGE FUNERAL CUSTOMS.

At Woodbridge the burial feast is called mulled-ale. Mr. Redstone suggests that this is a corruption of mould-ale. The dying person chooses what the bearers shall drink.

The bearers all drink before they go to the church ; the mourners drink afterwards.

All the mourners attend church on the Sunday after the funeral. People who otherwise never go to church do not fail to attend on this occasion. There is a common belief that the clergyman is obliged to preach a sermon from any text that the mourners may choose; and there is an instance cited of a man who paid the clergyman a guinea and insisted upon exercising this right.

From Mr. Redstone.

Salt.—The practice of setting a plate of salt on the breast of a corpse prevails generally in East Anglia, as it is said to do in Scotland; but tradition furnishes no account of the origin of the custom.

Forby. "Vocabulary of East Anglia," vol. ii, p. 426.

A 'GARLAND.'

" Yet here she is allowed her virgin crants."

Hamlet—Act v, Scene I.

From a letter from Miss Hawker. . . . "The church at Walsham-le-Willows is one of the few that contains a 'garland,'* or little suspended monument to a girl who died of a broken heart."

From a letter from Miss Gordon, sister of the vicar of Walsham-le-Willows. . . . "We have failed to find any information about Mary Boyce and her romantic memorial except what is most vague. An old woman, now dead, told me she remembered going with her mother to decorate it with flowers."

The "garland" in the parish church of Walsham-le-Willows hangs from the south wall of the nave. It is a large oval lozenge

---

* "But since I'm resolved to die for my dear
 I'll chuse six young virgins my coffin to bear;
 And all those young virgins I now do chase,
 Instead of green ribbands, green ribbands, green ribbands,
 Instead of green ribbands a garland shall wear;
 And when in the church in my grave I lie deep,
 Let all those fine garlands, fine garlands, fine garlands,
 Let all those fine garlands hang over my feet.
 And when any of my sex behold the sight,
 They may see I've been constant, been constant,
 They may see I've been constant to my heart's delight."

Ballad quoted in Chambers's "Book of Days," vol. i, p. 273.

surmounted by a small heart. On the side facing the chancel is written the name of Mary Boyce in plain black letters. Above the name are cross bones, and a skull and arrow, thus:

Below is a heart and arrow, thus:

On the side facing the west door is written:

Y̊ 15

NOVE

MBER

1685

In the baptismal register for 1665 there is the entry:

Mary, yᵉ daughter of William Boyce and Mary his wife, was baptised October yᵉ 29th."

In the burial register for 1685:

"Mary, yᵉ daughter of William Boyce, Nov., 15th."

[The Rev. C. D. Gordon, vicar of Walsham-le-Willows.

IX.—GAMES.

A *ball** custom now prevails annually at Bury St. Edmund's, Suffolk. On Shrove Tuesday, Easter Monday, and the Whitsuntide festivals, twelve old women side off for a game at trap and ball, which is kept up with the greatest spirit and vigour until sunset. One old lady, named Gill, upwards of sixty years of age, has been celebrated as the "mistress of the sport" for a number

---

* See similar custom among women in Chester on Easter Day.—" Chambers Book of Days," vol. i, p. 428.

of years past; and it affords much of the good old humour to flow round, whilst the merry combatants dexterously hurl the giddy ball to and fro. Afterwards they retire to their homes, where

> " Voice, fiddle, or flute,
> No longer is mute,"

and close the day with apportioned mirth and merriment.

Communicated by S. R. to W. Hone's " Everyday Book," vol. i, p. 430.

SUFFOLK GAMES.

Omitting games so universal as cricket, leap-frog, marbles, etc.— we have All the birds in the air, and All the fishes in the sea— bandy, bandy-ricket, base-ball, brandy-ball, bubble-hole, bull in the park (this I suspect to be the same as frog in the middle), blind-hob, blind man's buff, bob-cherry, bos, buck, buck, how many horns do I hold up?—cross questions and crooked answers, cross bars, cat after the mouse—dropping the letter, dumb crambo, Dutch concert—English and French—French and English (different games) —frog in the middle (see bull in the park), follow my leader, football, five stones—gull—handkerchiefs, hats, hide and find, hie co-colorum jig, hitchy cock ho, hocky, hog over hie, honey pots, hop scotch, horny hic, hot cockles, hunt the slipper—I spy I— Jack's alive, Jack be nimble, Jib Job Jeremiah—kick the bucket— my lady's toilet, magical music—niddy noddy, nine holes—oranges and lemons—prisoner's base, poor tanner, prison bars, plum pudding and roast beef, puss in the corner—rakes and roans, robbers— salt eel, snap dragon, snap apple—threading the tailor's needle, Tom Tickler's ground, three jolly butchers,—what's my thought like, work at one as I do.

Ed. Moor. " Suffolk Words and Phrases," p. 238.

Camp,* s. an ancient athletic game at Ball, now almost super-

---

* A much more detailed account of Camp is given in Moor's " Suffolk Words and Phrases," from which it appears to be substantially the same game as Rugby Football.—C. G.

seded by cricket, a less hardy and dangerous sport. . . . Two
varieties are at present expressly recognised ; *rough-play* and
civil-play. In the latter there is no boxing. But the following
is a general description of it as it was of old, and in some places
still continues. Two goals are pitched at the distance of 120
yards from each other. In a line with each are ranged the combatants. . . . The number on each side is equal; not always the
same, but very commonly twelve. They ought to be uniformly,
dressed in light flannel jackets, distinguished by colours. The ball
is deposited exactly in the mid-way. The sign or word is given
by an umpire. The two sides, as they are called, rush forward.
The sturdiest and most active of each encounter those of the other.
The contest for the ball begins and never ends without black
eyes and bloody noses, broken heads or shins, and some serious
mischiefs. If the ball can be carried, kicked or thrown to one of
the goals, in spite of all the resistance of the other party, it is
reckoned for one towards the game, which has sometimes been
known to last two or three hours. But the exertion and fatigue
of this is excessive. So the victory is not always decided by
number of points, but the game is placed against time as the
phrase is. It is common to limit it to half an hour. . . . The
prizes are commonly hats, gloves, shoes, or small sums of money.
. . . Ray says that in his time, this ancient game prevailed most
in Norfolk, Suffolk, and Essex. . . . A. S. Campian, præliari.

Camping-land, s. a piece of ground set apart for the exercise of
camping-land was given for this purpose with all legal formalities.
. . . In the late Sir John Cullum's "History of Hawsted, in
Suffolk," the *camping-pightle* is mentioned under the date 1466.
A large piece of pasture land at Stowmarket is still called the
camping-land. Other instances might be mentioned in other parishes
in both counties. (Norfolk and Suffolk.)

Forby. "Vocab. of E. Anglia," vol. i, p. 51.

Kit-Cat.—A game played by boys. . . . Three small holes are
made in the ground triangularly, about twenty feet apart, to mark
the position of as many boys, who each holds a small stick about

two feet long. Three other boys of the adverse side pitch succes-
sively a piece of stick, a little bigger than one's thumb called
cat, to be struck by those holding the sticks. On its being struck,
the boys run from hole to hole dipping the ends of their sticks in
as they pass, and counting, one, two, three, etc., as they do so,
up to 31, which is game. Or the greater number of holes gained
in the innings may indicate the winners as at cricket.

Kit-Cat Cannis.—A sedentary game, played by two, with slate
and pencil. . . . It is won by the party who can first get three
marks (o's or x's) in a line. . . .

Ed. Moor. "Suffolk Words and Phrases," p. 200.

Salt eel.—One of our numerous recreations. . . . This is something
like *hide and find*. The name of salt eel may have been given
it from one of the points of the game, which is to *baste* the
runaway individual whom you may overtake, all the way home
with your hankerchief twisted hard for that purpose. *Salt eel*
implies on board ship, a rope's ending, and on shore, an equivalent
process. "Yeow shall have *salt eel* for supper," is an emphatic
threat. . . .

Ibid. p. 328.

Laugh-and-lay-down, s. a childish game at cards, in which the
player, who holds a certain combination of cards, lays them down
on the table and is supposed to *laugh* at his success in winning
the stake.

Forby. "Vocabulary of East Anglia," vol. ii, p. 192.

Morris, s. an ancient game, in very common modern use. In
Shakespear's Midsummer Night's Dream, it is called "nine men's
morris" from its being played with nine men as they were then,
and still are now called. We call it simply *morris*. Probably
it took the name from a fancied resemblance to a dance, in the
motions of the men. . . . Shepherd's boys and other clowns

play it on the green turf, or on the bare ground ; cutting or
scratching the lines, on the one or the other. . . . In towns,
porters and other labourers play it, at their leisure hours, on the
flat pavement, tracing the figure with chalk. It is also a domestic
game; and the figure is to be found on the back of some draught-
boards. . . . On the ground, the men are pebbles, broken tiles,
shells, or potsherds ; on a table, the same as are used at draughts
or back-gammon.

Ibid. vol. ii, p. 220.

Nine-Holes, s. pl. A rustic game ; or indeed more than one.
In one of them, nine round holes are made in the ground, and
a ball aimed at them from a certain distance. This is supposed
in Nare's Glossary to be the modern form (whether subject to the
same rule of playing or not) of the " Nine men's morris,"
mentioned by Shakespear. We have that game, and it is different,
being played on a flat surface. In our other game of *nine-holes,*
the holes are made in a board with a number over each, through
one of which the ball is to pass. This must be something like
Trou-madame (of which, indeed, there are many varieties or
resemblances), only that it is played on the ground, and in the
open air.

Ibid. vol. ii, p. 232.

One and thirty, a game at cards, much resembling vingt-un,
but of very venerable antiquity, assuredly, for it is alluded to
by Bishop Latimer in one of his sermons. It was many years
ago called *one and thirty* turntail, and *one and thirty* bone-ace.
The first name was from turning up the last drawn card, to shew
whether the number was exactly made up or exceeded ; the second,
from the fortunate contingency of drawing an ace after two tens ;
the ace, counted for eleven, made up the game, and was certainly
a good ace. It is still played by children.

Ibid. vol. ii, p. 238.

Bandy-Hoshoe, s. a game at ball played with a *bandy* either made of some very tough wood, or shod with metal, or with the point of the horn or the hoof of some animal. The ball is a knob or knarl from the trunk of a tree, carefully formed into a globular shape. The adverse parties strive to beat it with their *bandies*, through one or other of the goals placed at proper distances. It is probably named from the supposed resemblance of the lower end of the *bandy*, in strength or curvature, to a horse-shoe; or it may be so called from being shod, as it were, with horn or hoof. In particular, the empty hoof of a sheep or calf, which is frequently used, may be well assimilated to a shoe.

Ibid. vol. i, p. 14.

Blind-Sim, *Blind-Hob*, s. the game of blind-man's buff. The unfortunate wight whose lot it is to be hood-winked, and who is thumped and punched by the other players, bears the contemptuous name of a coarse clown; to make fun for the company as in a pantomime.

Ibid. vol. i, p. 28.

Ducks and Drakes.—A boyish pastime, played by casting stones on to the surface of a still piece of water, slantingly, that they may dip and emerge several times. If once, it is "a duck"—if twice, "a duck an a drake"—if thrice, "a duck an a drake an a fie'penny cake"—four times, is "a duck an a drake an a fie'penny cake an a penny to pah the baker." If more than four, "a duck" —"a duck an a drake," etc., are added. These distinctions are iterated quickly to correspond in time, as nearly as may be, with the dips of the stone.

Ed. Moor. "Suffolk Words and Phrases," p. 115.

Fighting Cocks, s. pl. the spikes of the different species of plaintain, with which boys play a game so called.

Forby. "Vocab. of E. Anglia," vol. i. p. 113. *See* Moor, p. 84.

CHILDREN'S GAMES, COMMUNICATED BY MISS NINA LAYARD, IPSWICH.

I.

Make a Ring.

The girls are named all round with different colours. Then one says 'The police of the parish has lost his cap, some say this and some say that, but I say Mr. —— cap.' Then the girl answers quickly 'Me Sir.' Then the other answers, 'Yes you Sir.' The girl answers 'Not me Sir.' Then she says, 'Who then, Sir?' The suspected girl answers 'Mr. —— Cap.'

You must answer quickly else you have to give a forfeit.

II.

'There's a Lady on the Mountain.'

Make a ring with one girl in the middle and sing :—

> "There's a lady on the mountain,
> Who she is I do not know;
> All she want is gold and silver;
> All she want is a nice young man.
> Now you're married you must be good,
> Make your husband chop the wood.
> Chop it fine and bring it in,
> Give three kisses in the ring."

III.

A number of girls stand in a line. Three girls out of the number represent Mother, Jack, and Daughter. Then mother leaves her children in charge of her daughter, counts them and says the following :—

> "I am going into the garden to gather some rue,
> And mind old Jack-daw don't get you,
> Especially you my daughter Sue,
> I'll beat you till you're black and blue."

While the mother is gone Jack comes and asks for a match which he takes, and hides her up. Then mother comes back, and counts her children and finds one missing. Then she asks where she is, and the daughter says that Jack has got her. Then mother beats daughter, and leaves them again saying the same words as before until the children have gone.

IV.

Make a Ring.

All stand in a line with two girls at the end. One girl says:—
'How many miles to London?'

Ans. 'Three score ten.'

Girl. 'Can I get there by candle-light?'

Ans. 'Yes, and back again.'

Girl. 'Open the gate and let me through.'

Ans. 'Not unless you're black and blue.'

Girl. 'Here's my black and here's my blue.'

*Ans. 'Open the gates and let me through.'

All say. 'Dan, Dan, thread the needle, Dan, Dan, sew.

(Keep repeating.)

Miss Layard adds the following notes and suggestions. 'This seemed to me interesting because it is essentially a Suffolk game (if not Ipswich) because of the distance to London. Can the gate refer to the gate of the old town wall? Have the colours black and blue any significance?'

V.

'*The Tower of Barbaree.*'

Two girls join hands; some of the girls representing soldiers come and ask them if they will surrender the Tower of Barbaree. The others answer, 'We won't surrender, we won't surrender the Tower of Barbaree.' Then the girls say: 'We will go and tell the Queen, go and tell the Queen of Barbaree.' The girls answer: 'Don't care for the Queen, don't care for the Queen, the Queen of Barbaree.' A girl goes to the Queen, and says, 'Good morning young Queen, Good morning young Queen, I have a complaint to thee.'

The Queen says, 'Pray what is your complaint to me?'

The girl says, 'They won't surrender, etc.'

The Queen says, 'Take one of my brave soldiers.'

---

* Ought not this to be 'Open the gates and let her through?'

Then the soldier goes and jumps on the girls' hands to see
if they can break them apart. If they cannot, they do not have
the tower, but if they can break them they have the tower.

VI.

Make a ring with one girl in the middle; all join hands;
then sing:

> ' Golden apple, lemon and a pear,
> Bunch of roses she shall wear,
> Golden and silver by her side,
> I know who shall be her bride.
> Take her by the lily white hand,
> Lead her cross the water,
> Give her kisses one, two, three,
> Mrs. Gilburn's daughter.
> Now you're married, I wish you joy,
> Father and mother you must obey,
> Love one another like sister and brother,
> And now's the time to kiss away.'

VII.

Make a ring; all join hands and sing:

> ' How do you Luby Lue?
> How do you Luby Lue?
> How do you Luby Lue
> O'er the Saturday night.
> Put your right hand in,
> Put your right hand out,
> Shake it in the middle, and turn yourselves about.
> How do you Luby Lue? etc.'

Repeat this, naming " your left hand," " your right foot,"
" your heads," in turn, each with the refrain ' How do you Luby
Lue?' etc. In the last verse you are told to ' Put yourselves
in,' etc.

VIII.

Make a Ring.

All join hands, enclosing a boy and girl, the boy standing a
distance from the girl. The boy is called a gentleman, and the
girl a lady.

Gentleman :

> " There stands a lady on yonder hill,
> Who she is I cannot tell;
> I'll go and court her for her beauty
> Whether she answers me yes or no.
> Madam I bow *ounce* to thee."

Lady : 'Sir, have I done thee any harm?'

Gentleman : 'Coxconian.'

Lady : 'Coxconian is not my name, 'tis Hers and Kers and Willis and Cave.'

Gentleman : 'Stab me Ha! Ha! little I fear, over the waters there are but nine, I'll meet you a man alive. Over the waters there are but ten, I'll meet you there five thousand.'

Then the gentleman pretends to stab the lady, and she falls on the ground. Then he walks round the lady and sings:

> ' Rise up, rise up, my pretty fair maid,
> You're only in a trance;
> Rise up, rise up, my pretty fair maid,
> And we will have a dance.'

Then he lifts up the lady and the game is finished.

IX.

Make a ring with one girl in the centre. One goes round outside and the girl in the centre says:

' Who is going round my little stony wall?'

The girl outside answers

' Only little Johnny Lingo.'

Centre girl. ' Don't you steal any of my fat sheep.'

Outside girl. ' I stole one last night and gave it a little hay and away came a dickey-bird and stole another one.'

The outside girl takes one away each time, till they are all taken, and she hides them.

Centre girl asks the outside one for her sheep.

Outside girl. ' They are gone to the Blue House.'

Centre girl. ' They are not there.'

Outside girl. ' They are gone to the Red House.'

Centre. 'They are not there, I must come in.'

Outside. 'Your shoes are dirty.'

Centre. 'I can take them off.'

Outside. 'Your stockings are dirty.'

Centre. 'I can take them off.'

Outside. 'Your feet are dirty.'

Centre. 'I can cut them off.'

Outside. 'The blood will run.'

Centre. 'Wrap them up in blankets.'

Outside. 'It will soak through.'

Centre. 'I must come in.'

So she goes from side to side until they are caught.

[All these were taken down from the lips of the girls by Miss King, and given by her, together with the girls' names and addresses, to Miss Layard.]

GAMES PLAYED IN GRUNDISBURGH.

Taken down from a Grundisburgh girl's description by Camilla Gurdon.

I.

Mary is Weeping.

Form a ring. A child in the middle kneels and pretends to be weeping. The others sing:

> Poor Mary is a weeping, a weeping, a weeping,
> Poor Mary is a weeping on a fine summer's day.
> What is she weeping for, weeping for, weeping for,
> What is she weeping for on a fine summer's day?
>
> She's weeping for her sweetheart, etc.,
> She's weeping for her sweetheart on a fine summer's day.
>
> Pray get up and choose one, etc.,
> Pray get up and choose one on a fine summer's day.

Then she chooses one, whichever child she pleases. The ring of children divide to let the two pass out, and the ring sings:

> Pray go to church love, etc.,
> Pray go to church love on a fine summer's day.
>
> Pray put the ring on, etc.,
> Pray put the ring on on a fine summer's day.

Then the ring of children divides again to let the two into the middle, and sings:

> Pray come back love, etc.,
> Pray come back love on a fine summer's day.

> Now you're married we wish you joy,
> Your father and mother you must obey,*
> Love one another like sister and brother,
> And now its time to go away.

II.

Wall-flowers.

Form a ring. One child remains outside. The ring of children sing:

> Wall-flowers, Wall-flowers,
> Growing up so high
> All ye young maidens
> Are all fit to die.

The child outside says:

> Excepting (*names one*), and she's the worst of all,
> She can hop and she can skip,
> And she can turn the candle-stick.
> Fye! Fye! For shame,
> Turn your face to the wall again.

Then the child addressed turns round and looks the other way. This is repeated until all the children are named.

III.

The Poor Widow.

Form a ring, with one child in the middle. The ring of children sings:

> One poor widow is left alone, all alone, all alone,
> Choose the worst and choose the best,
> And choose the one that you like best.

Then the child in the middle chooses one, and the ring of children sings:

> Now she's married I wish her joy,
> Her father and mother she must obey,
> Love one another like sisters and brothers,
> And now it's time to go away.

* " First a girl and then a boy " is another version.—E.C.

Then the child who was first in the middle goes out, and the child that she chose stays in, and represents the poor widow *da Capo.*

IV.

The Jolly Miller.

The children sit in a ring and sing:

> There were three jolly millers (repeat 3 times)
> Down by the River Dee.
> One finger, one thumb, keep moving (repeat 3 times)
> Down by the River Dee.
> There were three jolly millers (3 times)
> Down by the River Dee.
>
> Two fingers, two thumbs, keep moving (3 times)
> Down by the River Dee.
> There were three, etc.

This formula is repeated, with an additional member each time until:

> Two fingers, two thumbs, one head, two arms,
> Two legs and one body keep moving,
> Down by the River Dee.

It is of course accompanied by appropriate gestures.

V.

Counting out Rhyme.

(From a Grundisburgh child.)

The girls each put their fingers on a cap, and then one says—putting her finger in the middle of the cap.

One (*takes her finger away*).

> Higgery Hoggery Heggery Am,
> Filsy Folsy Filsy Fam,
> Kuby Koby Virgin Mary,
> Sprinkle Sprinkle Blot.
> Out go she.

The girl to whom the last word, " she," comes, has to take her finger away.

X.—HARVEST CUSTOMS.

"In Suffolk," says Sir John Cullum in his entertaining History of Hawsted, "the harvest lasts about five weeks; during which the harvestman earns about £3. The agreement between the farmers and their hired harvestmen is made on Whitsun Monday. *Harvest gloves* of 7d. a pair are still presented. During harvest, if any strangers happen to come into the field, they are strongly solicited to make a present to the labourers, and those who refuse are reckoned churlish and covetous. This present is called a *Largess*; and the benefactor is celebrated on the spot, by the whole troop, who first cry out *Holla! Largess! Holla! Largess!* They then set up two violent screams, which are succeeded by a loud vociferation, continued as long as their breath will serve, and dying gradually away. Wheat harvest is finished by a little repast given by the farmer to his men. And the completion of the whole is crowned by a banquet, called the *Horkey*, to which the wives and children are also invited. The largess money furnishes another day of festivity, at the alehouse, when they experience to perfection the happiness of

Corda oblita laborum.

At all their merrymakings their benefactors are commemorated by *Holla! Largess!* The last load of corn is carried home, as it were, in triumph, adorned with a green bough."*

"In the descriptive Ballad which follows," says Bloomfield in his Advertisement to the "Horkey," "it will be evident that I have endeavoured to preserve the style of a gossip, and to transmit the memorial of a custom, the extent or antiquity of which I am not acquainted with, and pretend not to enquire into."

In Suffolk husbandry, the man who (whether by merit or by sufferance I know not) goes foremost through the harvest with the scythe or the sickle, is honoured with the title of '*Lord*,' and at the Horkey or harvest-home feast, collects what he can for himself and brethren from the farmers and visitors, to make a 'frolic' afterwards

---

* For the significance of this custom, cf. Frazer's *Golden Bough*, vol. i. 336–338; 340–346; 408; ii. 4, 7, 8, 68.

called 'the largess spending.' By way of returning thanks, though
perhaps formerly of much more, or of different signification, they
immediately leave the seat of festivity, and with a very long and
repeated shout of a 'largess' (the number of shouts being regulated
by the sums given) seem to wish to make themselves heard by the
people of the surrounding farms. And before they rejoin the company
within, the pranks and jollity I have endeavoured to describe usually
take place. These customs, I believe, are fast going out of use, which
is one great reason for my trying to tell the rising race of mankind
that such were the customs when I was a boy."—*The Suffolk Garland*,
printed and sold by John Raw, MDCCCXVIII., p 337.

They used to put green boughs and flowers, and sometimes a man
would put a ribbon, on the last load. They used to deck the last
sheaf with a green bough and put ta on top o' the load.

[Taken down from an old labourer's account of harvests in Suffolk
in old days. Grundisburgh.]

One of the Five Hundred points of Husbandry relates to August.

> Grant harvest-lord more, by a penny or twoo,
> To call on his fellowes the better to doo:
> Give gloves * to thy reapers a Larges to crie,
> And daily to loiterers have a good eie.—*Tusser*.

W. Hone. "Everyday Book," vol. ii, p. 1156.

Largess, s. a gift to reapers in harvest. When they have received
it, they shout thrice, the words "hallo largess;" an obvious corruption of the words "à la largesse," a very ancient form of soliciting
bounty from the great; not of thanking them for it. . . . . .
it is unquestionably a remnant of high feudal antiquity. It is called
halloing a *largess*."

> "The Vocabulary of East Anglia," by Rev. R. Forby,
> vol. ii, p. 190.

The custom after harvest of crying *largesse* prevails generally among
the people in this neighbourhood; but the *hockay*, or harvest-home,
since the introduction of task-work at the reaping season, begins to

---

* See the custom of giving gloves to servants at Lammas under " Miscellaneous
Customs."

fall into disuse. When this good old custom is kept here with due solemnity, besides the usual homage paid to the master and mistress of the house, a ceremony takes place which affords much mirth : a pair of ram's-horns, painted, and decorated with flowers, is carried in triumph round the festive board ; and as the forester who had killed the deer was honoured of old with the buck's horns, and saluted with a ditty—("As you like it," iv., 2)—so the harvest-man of Hengrave, having finished his labours, is crowned with the ram's horns, and greeted with a song which has the same point as the other, though more coarsely expressed.

"Gage's Hengrave," p. 7.

The time for hearing real Suffolk songs is after harvest, when the Hawkey time has come and the men have the supper so long looked forward to. They like it best arranged as their fathers have had it from time immemorial. A favourite song is a very short one. After the usual pressing from the "Lord of the Faist," one of the company will stand up and begin with :

> " Laarn tew be wise
> Laaaaren teeeew be wise,
> Larrrrrren tu beeeeeee wise ! "

This goes on till a voice calls out, " Will, come, dew you guv us more than that there, man, co'!" No notice, however, is taken by the singer of the remark, and he goes on, only varying the stress laid upon the words of each line. But at last the "Dew yow's" become general, when the singer coolly sits down, saying with an air of authority, " Larn that FUST."

Cambridge. "Brother Mike," Suffolk Notes & Queries, Ipswich Journal, 1877.

Healths.

The Master's Good Health.

Here's a health unto our Master, the founder of the feast,
I wish with all my heart and soul, in heaven he may find rest.
I hope all things may prosper, that ever he takes in hand,
For we are all his servants, and all at his command.
Drink, boys, drink, and see you do not spill ;
For if you do, you must drink two ; it is your master's will.

The Mistress's Good Health.

Now harvest is ended, and supper is past,
Here's our mistress's good health, boys, in a full flowing glass.
She is a good woman, she prepar'd us good cheer,
Come, all my brave boys, now and drink off your beer.
Drink, my boys, drink, till you come unto me,
The longer we sit, my boys, the merrier we shall be.

Sung on taking the Ale out of doors.

In yon green wood, there lies an old fox,
Close by his den, you may catch him or no.
His beard and his brush are all of one colour,

        (*Takes the glass and drinks it off.*)

I am sorry, kind sir, that your glass is no fuller.
'Tis down the red lane, 'tis down the red lane,
So merrily hunt the fox down the red lane.

Health to the Barley Mow.

Here's a health to the barley mow,
Here's a health to the man,
Who very well can
Both harrow, and plough, and sow.
When it is well sown,
See it is well mown,
Both raked, and gavell'd clean;
And a barn to lay it in,
Here's a health to the man,
Who very well can
Both thrash, and fan it clean.

To the Duke of Norfolk.*

I am the Duke of Norfolk,
Newly come to Suffolk,
Say, shall I be attended
Or no, no, no?
Good Duke, be not offended,
And you shall be attended,
You shall be attended
Now, now, now.

" The Suffolk Garland," 1818, pp. 401-402.

---

* At the " Harvest Supper," one of the guests is crowned with an inverted *pillow*,
and a jug of ale is presented to him by another of the company, kneeling. . . .
This custom has most probably some allusion to the homage formerly paid to the
Lords of Norfolk, the possessors of immense domains in this county.

. . . To 'serve the Duke of Norfolk' seems to have been equivalent to making merry, as in the following speech of mine host, at the end of the play of *The Merry Devil of Edmonton*, 1617 :

> 119. 'Why Sir George, send for Spindle's * noise presently,
> Ha ! ere't night *I'll serve the good Duke of Norfolk.*'

To which Sir John rejoins :

> ' Grass and hay ! mine host, let's live till we die,
> And be merry ; and there's an end.'
> —*Dodsley's Old Plays*, vol. v. p. 271.

Dr. Letherland, in a note which Stevens has printed on King Henry IV., part I, act ii., sc. 4 (where Falstaff says, " This chair shall be my State, this dagger my sceptre, and this *cushion my crown*,") observes that the country people in Warwickshire also use a *cushion* for a *crown*, at their harvest home diversions ; and in the play of King Edward IV., part II., 1649, is the following passage :

> ' Then comes a slave, one of those drunken sots,
> In with a tavern's reck'ning for a supplication,
> Disguised with a cushion on his head.'

" In the Suffolk custom, he who is crowned with the pillow is to take the ale, to raise it to his lips, and to drink it off without spilling it, or allowing the cushion to fall ; but there was, also, another drinking custom connected with this tune (*i.e.*, the tune to which ' I am the Duke of Norfolk,' was sung). In the first volume of *Wit and Mirth, or Pills to purge Melancholy*, 1698 and 1707, and the third volume 1719, is a song called *Bacchus' Health* ' to be sung by all the company, together with directions, to be observed.' They are as follows :

' First man stands up, with a glass in his hands, and sings :

> Here's a health to jolly Bacchus (sung three times),
> I-ho, I-ho, I-ho.
> For he doth make us merry (three times),
> I-ho, I-ho, I-ho ;
> *Come sit ye down together (three times),

(At this star all bow to each other and sit down.)

* Spindle's noise, *i.e.* Spindle's band, or company of musicians.

I-ho, I-ho, I-ho;
And bring † more liquor hither (three times),

(At this dagger all the company beckon the drawer)

I-ho, I-ho, I-ho.
It goes into the *cranium (three times),

(At this star the first man drinks his glass while the others sing
and point at him)

I-ho, I-ho, I-ho;
And † thou'rt a boon companion (three times),

(At this dagger all sit down, each clapping the next man on the
shoulder)

I-ho, I-ho, I-ho.

Every line of the above is to be sung three times, except I-ho,
I-ho, I-ho. Then the second man takes his glass and sings; and so
round."

> From vol. i, p. 118, of "The Ballad Literature and
> Popular Music of the Olden Time," by W. Chappell,
> F.S.A. Quoted by F.C.B., Suffolk Notes and
> Queries, Ipswich Journal, 1877.

XI.—LEGENDS: SPECTRAL, Etc.

GOLD BRIDGE.

The tradition . . . is as follows, and is current in the parish of
Hoxne to this day. In the hope of escaping his pursuers, the monarch
(Edmund) concealed himself under the arch of a bridge near the
place, now called Gold Bridge, and so named from the brilliant
appearance of the gilt spurs which he happened to wear, and which
proved the means of discovering his retreat. A newly-married
couple, returning home in the evening, and seeing by moonlight the

reflection of the spurs in the water, betrayed him to the Danes.
Indignant at their treachery, the king is said to have pronounced, in
the warmth of his resentment, a dreadful curse upon every couple
who should afterwards pass over this bridge on their way to or from
the altar of Hymen ; and we are told even at this day, after an
interval of nearly one thousand years, such is the superstitious regard
paid to this denunciation, that persons, proceeding to or coming from
the church on such an occasion, never fail to avoid the bridge, even if
they are obliged to take a circuitous road.

"The Suffolk Garland," p. 204.

It is thought that the King's bright armour is still to be seen
glimmering through the water of the brook.

"Handbook for Essex, Suffolk, Norfolk and Cambridgeshire," Murray, 1875, p. 183.

Martyrdom of St. Edmund.

The circumstances relating to St. Edmund, says the historian of
Bury, which took place on the retreat of the Danes, and which have
formed a favourite theme for the Monkish writers and a favourite
subject for their painters and sculptors, are given with miraculous
embellishments, and with various degrees of amplification by most of
the monastic poets and historians.

To offer the utmost indignity to the martyred King, the Pagans
cast his severed head and body into the thickest part of the woods at
Eglesdene. When the departure of the Danes removed the terror
which their presence had inspired, the East Anglians, prompted by
affection for their late Sovereign, assembled, in considerable numbers,
to pay his corpse the last duties of attachment. After a sorrowful
search the body was discovered, conveyed to the neighbouring village,
Hoxne, and there interred; but the head could not be found. These
zealous and dutiful subjects, therefore, divided themselves into small
parties, and searched every part of the wood. Terrified by its
thickness and obscurity, some of them cried out to their companions,
" Where are you?" A voice answered, " Here, here, here !" They
hastened to the place whence the sound proceeded, and found the

long-sought head in a thicket of thorns, guarded by a wolf, "an unkouth thyng and strange agwyn nature." The people, almost overpowered with joy, with all possible veneration, took the holy head, which its guardian quietly surrendered to them, and carried it to the body. The friendly wolf joined in the procession, and after seeing "the precious treasure," that he had with so much care protected, deposited with the body, returned into the woods with doleful mourning. The head was some time after observed to have united with the body; and the mark of separation appeared round the neck like a "purpil thread." His martyrdom is thus described by Langtoft:

. . . . , ...

> He attired him to bataile with folk that he had,
> But this cursed Danes so grete oste ay lad,
> That Edmund was taken and slayn at the last,
> Full far fro the body lay was the hede kast.
> The body son they fonde, the hede was in doute,
> Up and downe in the felde thei souht it aboute.
> To haf knowing thereof alle thei were in were,
> Till the hede himself said, Here, here, here!
> Ther thei fonde the hede is now a faire chapelle,
> Oxen hate the toun ther the body felle.
> Ther where he was schotte another chapelle standes
> And somewhat of that tree thei bond untille his hands,
> The tone is fro the tother moten a grete myle,
> So far bare a woulfe the hede and kept it a grete while,
> Until the hede said "Here," als I befor said,
> Fro the woulfe thee it toke, unto the body it laid,
> Men sais ther he ligges the flesh samen gede,
> But the token of the wonde als a red threde,
> Now lies he in schryne in gold that is rede,
> Seven yere was he Kyng that tyme that he was dede.

. . . .   The feast of St. Edmund, November the 20th, was ranked amongst the holydays of precept in this kingdom by the national Council of Oxford, in 1222, and was observed at Bury with the most splendid and joyous solemnities. We find that, upon this festival, 150 tapers of 1lb. weight or more illuminated the abbey church, its altars, and its windows. The "revel on St. Edmund's night" was of a character somewhat more noisy, turbulent and unhallowed; a loose being then given to every species of jollity and amusement.

"Suffolk Garland," p. 349.

In the year 1014 the tyrant Sweyn, after innumerable and cruel misdeeds, which he had been guilty of either in England or in other countries, to complete his own damnation, dared to exact a heavy tribute from the town where lies interred the uncorrupted body of the royal martyr Edmund, a thing that no one had dared to do before, from the time when that town had been given to the Church of the above-named Saint. He repeatedly threatened, also, that if it was not quickly paid, beyond a doubt, he would burn the town, together with the townsmen, utterly destroy the Church of the Martyr himself, and torment the clergy with various tortures. In addition to this he even dared to speak slightingly of the martyr himself, and to say that he was no saint at all. . . . At length, towards the evening of the day on which, in a general council he held at a place called Geagnesburt (Gainsborough), he had again repeated these threats, while surrounded with most numerous crowds of Danes, he alone beheld Saint Edmund coming armed towards him ; on seeing whom he was terrified, and began to cry out with loud shrieks, exclaiming, ' Fellow-soldiers, to the rescue, to the rescue ! behold St. Edmund has come to slay me;' after saying which, being pierced by the Saint with a spear, he fell from the throne upon which he was sitting, and suffering great torments until nightfall, on the third day before the mones of February, terminated his life by a shocking death."—*Riley's Roger de Hoveden's Annals.*

J. Varden. "East Anglian Handbook for 1865," p. 67.

Ghosts.

It is certainly very rare to find anyone who professes to have actually seen a ghost. Even in the neighbourhood of old castles, or of the ruins of religious houses, it is rather an indistinct terror that prevails, than a belief of any particular spectral appearance. We frequently hear of the vision of a " white woman " that haunts a particular spot; or of "a coach drawn by horses without heads;" but nobody pretends to assign a name to the lady, or to guess at the owner of the decapitated horses. The counties of Norfolk and Suffolk (and particularly the latter) are remarkable for the great number of old gentlemen's seats now, for the most part, degraded into farm houses. . . . Most of these are said to be haunted, but not by the ghost of any particular person. It is like a common rumour, which everybody has heard, but of which nobody knows the origin. The only instance of the identity of a ghost fairly established, that a pretty considerable research has been able to discover, is in a village on the coast at the eastern extremity of Suffolk; where there is still an existing memorial of the perturbed spirit. A seaman, it appears, of eccentric notions, died at an early age in the parish in question. During his life he had often told his relations that he would not be buried in the usual way, but insisted on being laid in the grave with his head to the East; and repeatedly assured them that, if he were buried otherwise he should not rest in peace. When he died, however, his family either forgot, or neglected his injunctions, and he was put into the ground in the accustomed manner. He had not been long buried before it was rumoured in the parish that the dead man was very unquiet; and several persons asserted that they had seen him wandering about the churchyard. The tale, as usual, gathered strength by circulation; and at length made so much noise, that his relations were induced to have the coffin taken up, and a new grave dug, a few feet distant from the former, in which he was laid in his favourite position with his head to the East. From this time he rested quietly. . . . His grave is still in existence . . . . with the head-stone at the East end of it. . . . It ought perhaps to be added that the date of this burial is before the middle of the last century.

Forby. " Vocabulary of E. Anglia," vol. ii, p. 412.

A Dutch prisoner at Woodbridge in Suffolk, in the reign of King Charles II., could discern Spirits; but others that stood by could not. The bell tolled for a man newly-deceased. The prisoner saw his phantom, and did describe him to the Parson of the parish, who was with him; exactly agreeing with the man for whom the bell tolled. Says the prisoner, now he is coming near to you, and now he is between you and the wall. The Parson was resolved to try it, and went to take the wall of him, and was thrown down; he could see nothing. This story is credibly told by several persons of belief.

"Miscellanies upon Various Subjects" by John Aubrey, Esq., F.R.S., London: printed for W. Otteridge, Strand; and E. Easton, at Salisbury. MDCCLXXXIV.

A DISFIGURED DIVELL.

Stephen Bateman, in his "Doome warning," published in 1582, relates that "Fishers toke a disfigured divell, in a certain *stoure* (which is a mighty gathering togither of waters from some narrow lake of the sea), a horrible monster with a goat's head, and eyes shyning lyke fyre, whereuppon they were all afrayde and ranne awaye; and that ghoste plunged himselfe under the ice, and running uppe and downe in the *stoure* made a terrible noyse and sound."

[Estuary of the River Stour in Suffolk?]

W. Hone. "Everyday Book," vol. i, p. 1299.

LEGENDS: SPECTRAL, ETC.

"Oulton High House, now a school, was built 1550, by the Hobarts; it retains a fine mantelpiece of the period, and some curious carved work. It was long known as the 'haunted house,' where some deeds of darkness had been committed, and at midnight a wild huntsman and his hounds, and a white lady carrying a poisoned cup, were believed to issue and to go their fiendish rounds. According to the legend, the spectre, in the time of George II., was the wife of a roystering squire, who, returning unexpectedly from the chase, surprised her toying with an officer, his guest, whose pity for her had ripened into guilty love. High words followed, and when the husband struck the vile suitor of his wife, the paramour drove his sword through his heart. The murderer and lady fled with her jewels and the gold of the murdered man. Years after, her daughter, who had been forgotten in the haste of departure, having grown up into a beautiful woman, was affianced to a young farmer of the neighbourhood. Being on the eve of marriage, she was sitting with him in the old hall one bleak November night, when a carriage, black as a hearse, its curtains closely drawn, and with servants dressed in sable liveries, stopped at the door. The masked men rushed in, and carried off the young girl to her unnatural mother, having stabbed the lover who had endeavoured in vain to rescue her. In a convent cemetery at Namur was a grave, said to cover the unhappy daughter who had been poisoned by her mother."

> Quoted from " A Guide to the Coasts of Essex, Suffolk and Norfolk," by Mackenzie E. C. Walcott (London : Edward Stanford, 1860), by X. M. T., Suffolk Notes and Queries, Ipswich Journal, 1877.

HEADLESS SPECTRES.

In the little village of Acton, Suffolk, a legend was current not many years ago, that on certain occasions, which, by the way, were never accurately defined, the park gates were wont to fly open at midnight "withouten hands," and a carriage drawn by four spectral horses, and accompanied by headless grooms and outriders, proceeded with great rapidity from the park to a spot called "the nursery corner." What became of the ghostly cortège at this spot, I have never been able to learn; but though the sight has not been seen by any of the present inhabitants, yet some of them have heard the noise of the headlong race. The "Corner" tradition says it is the spot where a very bloody engagement took place, in olden time, when the Romans were governors of England. A few coins have, I believe, been found, but nothing else confirmatory of the tale. Does history in any way support the story of the battle? Whilst writing on this subject, I may as well note, that near this haunted corner is a pool called Wimbell Pond, in which tradition says an iron chest of money is concealed : if any daring person ventures to approach the pond, and throw a stone into the water, it will ring against the chest; and a small white figure has been heard to cry in accents of distress, " That's mine !"

I send you these legends as I have heard them from the lips of my nurse, a native of the village.—W. Sparrow Simpson, B.A.—(vol. v, p. 195.)

> From *Choice Notes* (Folklore from Notes and Queries), 1889.

In Fornham All Saints' stood Babwell Priory. . . . There were four ancient mills in this parish, Wrenn's mill, Babbewell mill, the Lord's mill, and Stanworde's mill. The Mermaid pits are said to derive their name from the story of a love-sick maid, who perished here :

> Now there spreaden a rumour that everich night,
> The (*pitts*) ihaunted been by many a sprite,
> The miller avoucheth and all thereabout,
> That they full oft hearen the hellish rout.
>
> —*Chaucer*.

"The Hist. and Antiquities of Hengrave," by John Gage. Published by J. Carpenter, Old Bond St., 1822. p. 11.

THE SUFFOLK MIRACLE,

Being the Relation of a Young Man who after Death appeared to his Sweetheart, and carried her behind him *Forty Miles* in two Hours' Time, and was never seen after, but In The Grave.

Tune of "My Bleeding Heart," etc.

> A wonder strange as e'er was known,
> Than what I now shall treat upon,
> In Suffolk there did lately dwell,
> A Farmer rich, and known full well.

> He had a Daughter fair and bright,
> On whom he plac'd his chief delight,
> Her beauty was beyond compare,
> She was both virtuous and fair.

> A Young Man there was living by,
> Who was so charmed with her eye,
> That he could never be at rest,
> He was with Love so much possest.

> He made address to her. and she
> Did grant him Love immediately,
> Which when her Father came to hear,
> He parted her, and her poor dear.

> Forty miles distant was she sent,
> Unto her Uncle's with intent,
> That she should there so long remain,
> Till she had chang'd her mind again.

6

Hereat this young man sadly griev'd,
And knew not how to be reliev'd ;
He sigh'd and sobb'd continually,
That his true Love he could not see.

She by no means could to him send
Who was her heart's espoused Friend ;
He sigh'd, she griev'd, but all in vain,
For she confin'd must still remain.

He mourn'd so much, that Doctors' Art
Could give no ease unto his heart,
Who was so strangely terrify'd,
That in short t'me for Love he dy'd.

She that from him was sent away,
Knew nothing of his dying day,
But constant still she did remain ;
To Love the Dead was then in vain.

After he had in Grave been laid,
A month or more, unto this Maid
He came about middle of the night,
Who joy'd to see her heart's delight.

Her Father's Horse which she well knew,
Her Mother's Hood and Safeguard too,
He brought with him to testify
Her Parents' Order he came by.

Which when her Uncle understood,
He hop'd it might be for her Good,
And gave Consent to her straightway,
That with him she should come away.

When she was got her Love behind,
They pass'd as swift as any wind,
That in two Hours, or little more,
He brought her to her Father's Door.

But as they did this great haste make,
He did complain his head did ache ;
Her Handkerchief she then took out,
And ty'd the same his head about.

And unto him she thus did say,
Thou art as cold as any Clay,
When we get home a Fire we'll have,
But little dream't he went to Grave.

Soon were they at her Father's door,
And after she ne'er saw him more ;
I'll set the Horse up then, he said,
And there he left this harmless Maid.

She knocked, and straight amain, he cry'd
Who's there? 'tis I, she then reply'd :
Who wonder'd much her voice to hear,
And was possest with dread and fear.

Her Father she did tell, and then
He star'd like an affrighted Man,
Downstairs he ran, and when he saw her,
Cry'd out, my child, how cam'st thou here?

Pray Sir, did you not send for me,
By such a Messenger, said she,
Which made his Hair stand on his head,
As knowing well that he was dead.

Where is he then, to her he said,
He's in the Stable, quoth the Maid,
Go in, said he, and go to Bed,
I'll see the horse well littered.

He star'd about, and there could he
No shape of any Mankind see,
But found his Horse all in a sweat,
Which put him in a deadly fright.

His Daughter he said nothing to,
Nor no one else, though they well knew,
That he was dead a Month before,
For fear of grieving her full sore.

Her Father to his Father went,
(Who was decay'd) with this intent,
To tell him what his Daughter said,
So both came back unto this Maid.

They ask'd her, and she still did say,
'Twas him that then brought her away ;
Which when they heard they were amaz'd,
And on each other strangely gaz'd.

A Handkerchief, she said, she ty'd
About his head, and that they try'd ;
The Sexton they did speak unto,
That he the Grave would then undo.

Affrighted then they did behold,
His Body turning into Mould,
And tho' he had a Month boen dead,
This Handkerchief was about his Head.

This thing unto her then they told,
And the whole Truth they did unfold,
She was thereat so terrified,
And griev'd, she quickly after died.

Part not True Love, you Rich Men then,
But if they be right Honest Men,
Your Daughter's Love give them their way,
For Force oft breeds their Life's Decay.

From a "Broadside." *Loder, Printer, Woodbridge.*

THE WANDERING JEW.

This venerable personage still continues his wearisome pilgrimage. Nobody indeed professes to have seen him; but many have heard their grandmothers say that he appeared in their time. The circumstances of his history, as given by Mathew Paris, quoted by Brand, in the Appendix to his enlarged edition of Bourne's "Popular Antiquities" do not appear to be much known, and the wanderer is generally believed to be St. John, "tarrying till his Lord comes" (21st St. John, ver. 22.) . . . . His memory is now principally preserved in an allusive comparison. Of anyone, who is in unquiet motion from place to place, it is said, "He is as unsettled as the wandering Jew."

Forby. "Vocabulary of E. Anglia," vol. ii, p. 405.

Old Shock, s. a mischievous goblin, in the shape of a great dog, or of a calf, haunting highways and footpaths in the dark. Those who are so foolhardy as to encounter him, are sure to be at least thrown down and severely bruised, and it is well if they do not get their ancles sprained or broken; of which instances are recorded and believed.

Ib. vol. ii., p. 238.

Mork-shriek, s. a mockery; a humbug; a foolish old wife's tale. Literally, it means "a *shriek* in the dark." In some towns and villages "ghosts wilaid" still walk at the "witching time of night," and in various ways annoy the slumbering inhabitants; sometimes by piercing screams, "making night hideous" to dreaming old women and naughty children. But so much has the human mind been strengthened and improved in these happy days of general illumination, that the once terrific *mork-shriek* is become a mockery and a by-word among the vulgar.—Dan. *morck*, caligo.

Ib. vol. ii, p. 221.

Clim, s., a sort of imp which inhabits the chimneys of nurseries, and is sometimes called down to take away naughty children. He may perhaps have taken the name of " *Clym* of the Clough," the companion of Robin Hood, as the great Duke of Marlborough was for many years, and perhaps still is, the scarebabe of Flanders, under the name of Malbrouk.

Ib. vol. i, p. 67.

GALLEY TROT.

Galley Trot. This is the name of an apparition or cacodæmon, that has sorely frightened many people in the neighbourhood of Wood-bridge. It sometimes assumes the shape of a dog; and gives chase to those whose alarm compels them to run. Its appearance is sometimes as big as a bullock—generally white—and indefinable as to outline. Its haunts are more particularly at a place called Bath-slough, meaning a slough or bog in the parish of Burgh. But the place in question is not in, or very near, that parish, nor is there any slough. I can make nothing of the name; nor much of the story, though I have heard it related by more than one person who had suffered from the apparition.

Ed. Moor. " Suffolk Words and Phrases," p. 141.

" A STRANGE AND TERRIBLE WUNDER."

" Sunday, being the fourth of this August, in yͤ yeer of our Lord, 1577, to the amazing and singular astonishment of the present beholders, and absent hearers, at a certain towne called Bongay, not

1 1

past tenne miles distant from the citie of Norwiche, there fell from heaven an exceeding great and terrible tempest, sodein and violent, between nine of the clock in the morning and tenne of the day aforesaid.

. . . There were assembled at the same season, to hear divine service and common prayer, according to order, in the parish church of the said town of Bongay, the people thereabouts inhabiting, who were witnesses of the straungenes, the rarenesse and sodenesse of the storm, consisting of rain violently falling, fearful flashes of lightning, and terrible cracks of thūder, which came with such unwonted force and power, that to the perceiving of the people, at the time and in the place above named, assembled, the church did as it were quake and stagger, which struck into the hearts of those that were present, such a sore and sodain feare, that they were in a manner robbed of their right wits.

Immediately hereupō, there appeared in a most horrible similitude and likeness to the congregation then and there present, a dog as they might discerne it, of a black colour; at the sight whereof, togither with the fearful flashes of fire which then were seene, moved such admiration in the minds of the assemblie, that they thought doomes day was already come.

This black dog, or the divel in such a likeness (God hee knoweth al who worketh all), runing all along down the body of the church with great swiftnesse, and incredible haste among the people, in a visible fourm and shape, passed between two persons, as they were kneeling uppon their knees, and occupied in prayer as it seemed, wrung the necks of them bothe at one instant clene backward, insomuch that even at a momēt where they kneeled, they strāgely dyed.

This is a wōderful example of God's wrath, no doubt to terrifie us, that we might feare him for his iustice, or pulling back our footsteps from the pathes of sinne, to love him for his mercy.

To our matter again. There was at yᵉ same time another wonder wrought: for the same black dog, stil continuing and remaining in one and the self-same shape, passing by an other man of the congregation in the church, gave him such a gripe on the back, that therewith all he was presently drawn togither and shrunk up, as it

were a piece of lether scorched in a hot fire; or as the mouth of a
purse or bag drawen togither with a string.   The man, albeit hee was
in so straunge a taking, dyed not, but as it is thought is yet alive;
whiche thing is mervelous in the eyes of men, and offereth much
matter of amasing the minde.

Moreouer and beside this, the clark of the said church being
occupied in cleansing of the gutter of the church, with a violent
clap of thunder was smitten doune, and beside his fall had no further
harme: unto whom beeing all amased this straunge shape, whereof
we have before spoken, appeared, howbeit he escaped without
daunger: which might peradventure seem to sound against trueth,
and to be a thing incredible; but let us leave thus and thus to
iudge, and cry out with the prophet, O *Domine*, etc.—"O Lord, how
wonderful art thou in thy woorks."

 . . . . Now for the verifying of this report (which to sóe wil seem
absurd, although the sensiblenesse of the thing it self confirmeth it
to be a trueth) as testimonies and witnesses of the force which rested
in this straunge shaped thing, there are remaining in the stones of
the church, and likewise in the church dore which are mervelously
rēten and torne, yᵉ marks as it were of his clawes or talans.   Beside,
that all the wires, the wheeles, and other things belonging to the
clock, were wrung in sunder, and broken in peces.

And (which I should haue tolde you in the beginning of this report,
if I had regarded the obserring of order) at the time that this tempest
lasted, and while these storms endured, yᵉ whole church was so
darkened, yea with such a palpable darknesse, that one persone
could not perceive another, neither yet might discern any light at
all though it were lesser thē the least, but onely when yᵉ great
flashing of fire and lightning appeared.

These things are not lightly with silence to be overpassed, but
precisely and thoroughly to be considered.

On the self-same day, in like manner, into the parish church of
another towne called Blibery, not above sevē miles distant from
Bougay above said, the like thing Entred, in the same shape and
similitude, where placing himself uppon a maine balke or beam,
whereon some yᵉ Rood did stand, sodainely he gave a swinge downe

through ye church, and there also, as before, slew two men and
a lad, and burned the hand of another person that was there among
the rest of the company, of whom divers were blasted.

This mischief thus wrought, he flew with wonderful force to no
little feare of the assembly, out of the church in a hideous and
hellish likenes.

"A straunge and terrible Wunder wrought very late in the parish
Church of Bongay, a Town of no great distance from the citie of
Norwich, namely the fourth of this August in ye yeere of our Lord
1577, in a great tempest of violent raine, lightning, and thunder,
the like whereof hath been seldome seene. With the appearance
of an horrible shaped thing, sensibly perceiued of the people then
and there assembled. Drawen into a plain method, according to
the written copye by *Abraham Fleming*."

Hone's "Everyday Book," vol. i, p. 10.

It is worth mentioning here that the only incident in the whole
range of English history I have ever heard people of the labouring
class in this part of the country refer to, and I quite believe it is the
only incident tradition has preserved among them, is that of the
burning of Dr. Taylor, at Hadleigh, in the reign of Queen Mary.
. . . . I have sometimes heard the same person who had just spoken
of Dr. Taylor's martyrdom add : 'And at Framlingham Castle, bloody
Mary, who ordered Dr. Taylor's burning, was brought to bed of a
viper.' This is told with bated breath, and with an air and tone of
mystery to imply that the author of evil, the old Serpent, to whom
the wicked queen had sold herself, was the author of the viper.

"Some Materials for the Hist. of Wherstead," by F. B.
Zincke, p. 65.

Old Aldeburgh and also old Felixstowe now lie under the sea,
having been swallowed up; and it is fully believed that the church
bells may be heard, from time to time, sounding beneath the waters.

From Mr. Redstone.

The Wild Man of Orford.

Orford Castle.—At what Time, or by whom this Castle was built is not certain, the earliest Account being from King Henry I., Barth : Glanvill being then Governour of this Castle at wch Time some fishermen catch'd a wild Man in their Nets near this Place, all the parts of his Body resembled those of a Man; he had Hair on his Head, a long peaked Beard, and about ye Brest was exceeding hairy and rough.

> From a description of Orford Castle upon a Print: S. and N. Buck del et Sculp. Published according to Act of Parliament, March 25th, 1738—in the possession of Mr. J. Loder, Woodbridge.

A curious story relating to Orford is told by Ralph of Coggeshall (abbot of the monastery there in the early part of the 13th century). Some fishermen on this coast (A.D. 1161) caught in their nets one stormy day a monster resembling a man in size and form, bald-headed, but with a long beard. It was taken to the Governor of Orford Castle, and kept for some time, being fed on raw flesh and fish, which it " pressed with its hands " before eating. The soldiers in the Castle used to torture the unhappy monster in divers fashions " to make him speak ; " and on one occasion, when it was taken to the sea to disport itself therein, it broke through a triple barrier of nets and escaped. Strange to say, not long afterwards it returned of its own accord to its captivity ; but at last, " being wearied of living alone, it stole away to sea and was never more heard of." A tradition of this monster, known as " the wild man of Orford," still exists in the village.

> Grose. " Antiquities of England and Wales," vol. iii.; " Handbook " for Essex, Suffolk, etc. Murray, p. 153.

Friar Bungay.

I have a dateless time-worn old pamplet in small quarto, of twenty-four pages, " printed for B. Deacon, at the Angel Inn, Gilt Spur

L 1 *

Street, without Newgate," extracts from which I think will not be
without interest to some of your readers. It is entitled—" The most
famous History of the learned Fryer Bacon; showing his parentage
and Birth. How he came to be a Scholar and to study Art Magick:
with the many wonderful Things he did in his Life-time to the
Amazement of the whole World; in making a *Brazen Head*, to haue
Walled all *England* with Brass, With his Penitent Death. Also, the
Merry Waggeries of his Man Miles; and the Exploits of Vandermaster, a *German*; and *Fryer* Bungay, an *English* Conjuror. With
the manner of their woful Deaths, as a Warning to others."

 . . . . " A Gentleman in Oxfordshire being greatly enamoured of a
young gentlewoman, after long Courtship, got her Good Will, with
the consent of her Father. But whilst everything was preparing for
the Marriage, a rich Knight, who had a mind to the young Lady,
prevailed with the covetous Father to break off the Match, and marry
her to him. The young Gentleman was much grieved at this, and so
was the Lady, for she had now settled her affections entirely on him,
and was much averse to the Knight's courtship; whereupon he [the
Knight] consulted *Fryer Bungy* how to get her, promising him a great
Summ if he accomplished it. Why, says he, do but get her and her
Father to ride with you abroad in a coach, and which way soever
they direct or design to go, I will so enchant the Coachman and
Horse, that they shall directly pass to such an old chapel, where I
will be ready to marry you. This the Knight resolved to put into
practice, and it accordingly proceeded so far, that they did come to
the Chapel, found the Fryer there, and the Marriage was proposed.

 [The young lover applies to Friar Bacon who shows him in a
" Magick Glass " what is happening; Bacon strikes Bungay dumb,
rescues the lady and marries her to the Gentleman from Oxfordshire.]

 " After this, *Vandermaster*, the German Conjurer, came over into
England, and not daring to venture on *Bacon*, he thought to be
revenged on Bungy; so he privately challenged him into a Wood,
to Conjure, thinking to make his Spirit destroy him. They made
their circles, and *Vandermaster* raised a Dragon, which, running
round *Bungy's* circle, threw so much fire on him, that he almost
roasted him. *Bungy* raised a Sea-Monster, that with spouting Floods

almost drowned *Vandermaster*; and to destroy the Dragon, raised up the Spirit of *S. George*, while Vandermaster raised up that of *Perseus*, to destroy the Sea-Monster; and so they vanished.

"Then *Vandermaster* raised up *Hector*; and *Bungy* Achilles, who trained their Greeks and Trojans to the Battle, and fought so desperately that the whole Element seemed on fire; Thunder and Lightning, and such prodigious Storms ensued that the People for many miles distant, concluded the World was at an End; and the Spirits growing too strong for these Conjurors and their Charms, broke into their Circles, and tore them in a thousand pieces, scattering their Limbs about the Fields, and so ended they their miserable lives."

. . . Blomefield in his *History of Norfolk*, under the head of "Norwich," vol. iv, pp. 114–115, in speaking of men of worth and learning among the Franciscans says :—"1290. About this time died Brother Thomas de Bungeia or Bungye, who was born in the town of that name, which stood on an Island by the river *Waveney*, anciently called Le Bon Eye, or the *Good Island*. . . . Besides the common notions of Philosophy, he was also a great Mathematician, so knowing in the hidden secrets of nature, and so well skilled in uncommon experiments that he performed such wonders by his wit and art, as exceeded the understanding of the vulgar, and were not intelligible to some men of letters, and therefore the Doctor was traduced by some, as a person dealing in the black art, holding a correspondence with demons, and in a word a Conjuror, and one that had to do with the Devil."

Bungay, Aug. 19, 1868. G. B. Baker. "The East Anglian" or "Notes and Queries," edited by S. Tymms, vol. iii, p. 302.

" A SHOCK."

"In Melton stands the 'Horse and Groom'—in the days of toll-bar gates (thirty years ago) occupied by one Master Fisher. It was a dark night when Goodman Kemp of Woodbridge entered the inn in a hurried frightened manner, and asked for the loan of a gun to shoot a "Shock," which hung upon the toll-gate bars. It was a "thing" with a donkey's head and a smooth velvet hide. Kemp, somewhat emboldened by the support of companions, sought to grab the creature and take it to the inn to examine it. As he seized it, it turned suddenly round, snapped at Kemp's hand and vanished. Kemp bore the mark of the Shock's bite upon his thumb to his dying day."

> From Mr. Redstone. "Told by Fisher, the inn-keeper's son, aged 70."

"The place I know supposed to be haunted by "Shock" is where a man was pitched off a waggon and broke his neck, and his spirit is supposed to be periodically seen in the form of a calf or big dog with shaggy mane and tea-saucer eyes. The said creature is, I believe, only to be seen by those born during Chime hours (8, 12, 4), these people being also qualified to see any ghost. I do know one tale which is true—at least the man who saw firmly believes it, and was perfectly sober at the time. He was a carter, and driving one night by moon-light saw a funeral procession coming—mourning coaches, etc. As the road was narrow, he stopped and drew aside to let it pass, noticing how quietly it went by. Afterwards he made enquiries, and found that there was no funeral; but that on the anniversary of the death of some old chap who died long ago, the said procession was seen, and had been seen by others. The man who tells this was living at Pakenham at the time.

"Of course you know the screech owl superstition—the death of some near relation before the year is out. If you kill it you die yourself."

> Extract from a letter written to Mr. Redstone.

Neere unto it, [Aldeburgh] what time as in the yeare 1555, by reason of unseasonable weather the Corne throughout all England was choked and blasted in the eare, there grew Pease miraculously among the rocks, without any earth at all about them about the end of September, and brought down the price of Corne.

> Britain. By W. Camden, translated by Philemon Holland. London, 1637, p. 466.

Hermanus, a monk of St. Edmund's, who lived in the time of the Conqueror, recounts in his history of the Saint's miracles, how

Leofstan, Sheriff of the county of Suffolk under King Athelstan, was struck with instant madness in attempting to withdraw a culprit woman from the martyr's shrine, to which she had fled for sanctuary.

"Hist. and Antiquities of Suffolk," Thingoe Hundred, by J. Gage, p. 9.

HEADLESS HORSES.

At Boulge Hall, upon the stroke of twelve at midnight, a coach drawn by a pair of headless horses, and driven by a headless coachman, who dismounts to open the lodge gates, takes back the ghost of the late owner, Mr. FitzGerald. A man from Debach stayed up one night to see if it were true, and "he was wholly frighted by the sight."

From Mr. Redstone.

A FOOTLESS GHOST.

In years gone by there lived at Dallinghoo a Widow Shawe who committed suicide by cutting her throat. She now haunts the lanes and flits by without feet. She has been seen by many, and amongst those whom she has startled is Mrs. H., a thatcher's wife (my informant for this and other Dallinghoo tales). This person is a firm believer in ghosts, for she has seen spirits track the footsteps of her children.

A GHOST THAT CANNOT BE LAID.

Beneath a post of a high gate in Dallinghoo lies a hidden treasure ; the ghost of its former owner haunts the spot and twelve clergymen have unitedly failed to lay the spirit.

From Mr. Redstone.

WOOLPIT.

. . . In a meadow near the church is a large moated area, having in its centre a fine spring, called Lady's Well, said to possess medicinal virtues for the cure of sore eyes, and to have anciently had a chapel near it.

"Hist. Gazetteer and Directory of Suffolk," by W. White, Sheffield. W. White, Hoole's Chambers, Bank Street. 1885. p. 668.

"THE QUEEN OF HELL."

Boulge is said to be haunted by a **Mrs. Short**, who is called the "Queen of Hell." "She murdered a gentleman at Boulge Hall. The stain is on the floor where she murdered him. Now (that is 70 years after) she come out of the gate in a carriage with a pair of horses that have got no heads. She wears a silk dress. There is a light on the carriage, and a man drives the horses. About three years ago a servant girl lived there. Mrs. Short went into her room and pulled all her things off her. The girl said she felt it's (the ghost's) breath like a wolf upon her."

Copied from a written account given to Mr. Redstone.

Mrs. Smith-Debach. "She was a wicked woman. She lived 39 years ago. My mother and father have seen her run up and down the bank. She had a night dress and night cap on. She has been seen by several. There was a woman who went to shop one night, and saw her setting on the bank. The woman had a lantern in her hand. She held it up and said, ' I am not a-frightened if you are.' She turned round and looked in her face and so sanked away."

Ibid.

XII.—LOVE CHARMS AND TESTS.

The following spell is said to be still used by some country maidens in Suffolk :—

> "A clover of two, if you put in y^r shoe,
> The next man you meet in field or lane
> Will be y^r husband, or one of the name."

To ascertain whether her pretended lovers really love her or not, the maiden takes an apple pip, and naming one of her followers, puts the pip in the fire. If it makes a noise in bursting, from the heat, it is a proof of love; but if it is consumed without a crack, she is fully satisfied that there is no real regard towards her in the person named.

The kitchen-maid, when she shells green peas, never omits, when she finds one having *nine* peas, to lay it on the lintel of the kitchen door; and the first male who enters it is infallibly to be her husband, or at least her sweetheart.

If two people wish to marry, they must take the Church key and place it over the sixth and seventh verses of the eighth chapter of the Song of Solomon,—" Set me a seal upon thine heart, as a seal upon thine arm; for love is strong as death; jealousy is cruel as the grave; the coals thereof are coals of fire, which hath a most vehement flame. Many waters cannot quench love, neither can the floods drown it; if a man would give all the substance of his house for love, it would utterly be contemned."

Over the words they must hold the Church key, balancing it by the end; and if the wards of the key incline towards the verses, which by a skilful manipulation they can easily be made to do, it is a sign that the course of true love will run smooth.

But if after all, doubts of the lady's fitness to be his wife take possession of the gentleman's mind, there is another chapter in the Holy Bible, which, if consulted, will either confirm or scatter them. That chapter is the last in the Book of Proverbs. It contains thirty-one verses, corresponding with the number of days in the longest months. The hesitating lover must ascertain on what day of the month the birthday of the lady falls, and then compare with the verse which agrees with it in number. He will thus find out the kind of life which he will lead with her in the event of marriage; and if the verdict prove unfavourable, he will have an opportunity of avoiding a match which he has such strong reason to believe will not be a happy one.

Do not marry on Xmas day if two other couples are about to go through the sacred ceremony at the same time, for rest assured that if *three* couples marry on that day, at the same time, one of the party will certainly die during the ensuing year.

" The New Suffolk Garland," p. 175.

DIVINATION BY BIBLE AND KEY.

Any common bible, and any large key will answer the purpose. . . . It is resorted to by young women, for the purpose of ascertaining the first letter of their future husband's name. The mode of operation is as follows : the Key to be inserted between the leaves of the Bible, exactly over the 6th and 7th verses of the last chapter of Solomon's Song. The person who makes the inquiry is then to tie the bible closely together with the garter taken from her right knee ; and she and some other female are to suspend it, by placing each a finger under the bow of the Key. The enquirer is then to repeat the two verses to every letter of the alphabet, beginning with A, till she comes to the letter which is the initial of her future husband's name. As soon as she pronounces this happy letter, the bible will turn round. It will sometimes happen, that by awkwardness, or defect of management (for no want of good will can be supposed), the bible will obstinately refuse to move ; and whenever this is the case, the party inquiring is certainly destined to die an old maid.

> Forby. " Vocabulary of E. Anglia," Appendix, vol. ii, p. 399.

ST. MARK'S EVE.

There is another Vigil kept by young women on St. Mark's Eve, for the purpose of ascertaining their future husbands. Precisely at midnight the husband-seeker must go alone into the garden, taking with her some hemp-seed, which she is to sow, repeating at the same time the following lines :

> Hemp-seed I sow ;
> Hemp-seed, grow ;
> He that is my true love
> Come after me and mow.

It is believed that if this be done with full faith in the efficacy of the charm, the figure of the future husband will appear, with a scythe, and in the act of mowing.

> *Ib.* vol. ii, p. 408.

DUMB-CAKE.

On the same night, [St. Mark's Eve] and for the same purpose, [of ascertaining their future husbands] girls bake what is called the dumb-cake; which is made of the following ingredients:

> An egg-shell-full of salt,
> An egg-shell-full of wheat-meal,
> An egg-shell-full of barley-meal.

It must be baked before the fire, a little before twelve o'clock at night; the maker of the cake must be quite alone, must be fasting, and not a word must be spoken. At twelve o'clock exactly the sweet-heart will come in and turn the cake. The door must be left open, for a reason pretty obvious.

Ib. vol. ii, p 408.

ST. MARK'S EVE.

Two girls wash the hearthstone perfectly clean before going to bed, two clean pewter pots are "whelmed" down at the outermost corners, and then they (the girls, not the pewter pots) retire to their couch backwards, undressing and getting into bed backwards, and of course in perfect silence. In the morning they will find something under the pewter pots to tell them the trade of their future husband.

J. T. Varden. "E. A. Handbook," p. 124.

PLANTS OF OMEN.

The dandelion (*Leontodon Taraxacum*) is one of these. When its seeds are ripened they stand above the head of the plant in a globular form, with a feathery tuft at the end of each seed, and then are easily detached. The flower stalk must be plucked carefully, so as not to injure the globe of seeds, and you are then to blow off the seeds with your breath. So many puffs as are required to blow every seed clean off, so many years it will be before you are married.

Another plant of omen is the yarrow (*Achillæa millefolium*), called by us yarroway. The mode of divination is this: you must take one of the serrated leaves of the plant, and with it tickle the inside of the nostrils, repeating at the same time the following lines:

> " Yarroway, yarroway, bear a white blow,
> If my love love me, my nose will bleed now."

If the blood follows this charm, success in your courtship is held to be certain.

Forby. " Vocabulary of E. Anglia," vol. ii, p. 423.

If a break* is cut across, the veins are supposed to shew the initial of the name of the future husband or wife.

Ib. vol. ii, Appendix.

A Charm

To make a young woman seem to be in love with a young man.

Take new wax and the pouder of a dead man, make an image with the face downward and in the likeness of the person you wish to have : make it in the ouers of mars and in the new of the mone : under the left arm-poke place a Swaler's hart and a liver under the rite : you must have a new needal and a new thread : the Sprits name must be menchened, his sine and his character.

I take this opportunity to inform my frinds that about 16 years ago this Charm was put in practice by sum willains of witches at Needham-markett, William Studd been one of them : and they have put me to much torment and lamed me many times, they own to me that they make use of part of the bones of Mrs. Wilkerson of Felixstow, she that suffered at Rushmere sum years ago ; this is sartainly true, and I am ready to give it upon oth if required.—Tho. Colson.

Acts the 9 & 5. " It is hard for thee to kick against the pricks.

" The Suffolk Garland," 1818.

A similar superstition to that in Norfolk . . . was prevalent in Suffolk sixty or seventy years ago. I was not present at the scene

---

* Brakes, spl. fern. Forby. Vocab. of E. A., p. 37.

which I am about to describe, but heard it related by one who
lived in the house adjoining that in which it took place, and who
well knew all the circumstances of the case; and some of the
actors were known to myself.

Several young females determined, on some particular Eve, it
might be Allhallows, to silently watch a smock which they had
hung up on the back of a chair placed in the middle of a room,
in expectation that the lover of one of them would, at the hour of
midnight, appear and turn the garment. . . . . . .

Upwards of sixty-five years ago I was present when a young
female, the daughter of a respectable tradesman, came to an ancient
dame to enquire about an invocation to be said on St. Thomas's Eve.
The following is all that the old lady could remember of it; but
which she said was quite sufficient:—

> " Good St. Thomas, use me right,
> Bring to me my love this night,
> In his apparel, his array,
> The clothes he walks in every day."

Being very young at the time it was not thought that I should take
any notice of the matter; but there is an old Suffolk adage which
says " Little gotches* have great ears," and it was verified in this
case. . . . . The instructions how and when it should be repeated,
. . . . were as follows : The person was to get into bed backwards,
and repeat the words while doing so; but on no occasion was she. to
speak to anyone till the next morning. By following these directions
she might expect to dream of, and see in her dream, the person who
was to be her husband. I saw her again the following evening, when
she was questioned as to the result.; she made no confession further
than that she dreamed of one who wore *trowsers* (breeches were in
vogue then), and that was construed to mean that she saw, or
imagined she saw, a young man who was well-known to be her
walking companion.

East Anglian. " Suffolk Notes and Queries." Ipswich
Journal, 1877.

* Gotch, a jug or pitcher with one ear or handle.—Moor. " Suffolk Words and
Phrases," p. 154.

Maidens anxious for husbands keep watch on Christmas Eve. She who wishes for a sight of her future spouse washes out her chemise, hangs it before the fire to dry and waits in solemn silence until midnight, when he will come in and turn the linen. This ceremony is also observed in some places on New Year's Eve. . . . Sometimes on New Year's Eve *four* girls prepare supper for five, then sitting each in a corner of the room till midnight, when the future husband of one of them comes in to supper.

J. T. Varden. "E. A. Handbook," p. 131.

To ascertain whether her pretended lovers really love her or not, the maiden takes an apple-pip, and naming one of her followers, puts the pip in the fire. If it makes a noise in bursting, from the heat, it is a proof of love; but if it is consumed without a crack, she is fully satisfied that there is no real regard towards her in the person named.

"The New Suffolk Garland," p. 176.

A knife thrust violently into the post at the foot of the bed accompanied with the following rhymes—

> It's not this post alone I stick,
> But (*lover's name*) heart I wish to prick;
> Whether he be asleep or awake,
> I'd have him back to me and speak.

—is supposed to bring the sulkiest of lovers back to his mistress.

J. T. Varley. "E. A. Handbook for 1885," p. 99.

To gain information concerning their future husbands, young maidens repeat the following charm on three consecutive Friday nights:—

> To-night, to-night is Friday night,
> Lay me down in dirty white,
> Dream who my husband is to be,
> Lay my children by my side
> If I am to live to be his bride.

On the last night the anxious one dreams of her future spouse. . . . Again the expectant one writes several male Christian names, and also her own, on slips of paper, rolls each separately in a little ball of clay, and then places them all in a pail of water. As the clay dissolves the slips are liberated, and the first that reaches the top is that of her future husband, but should her own win the race, she is placed for good and all upon the "old maid's list."

Ib. p. 109.

Wedding cake is in great request, as a small portion which has been drawn through the bridal ring placed on the pillow causes a maiden to dream of her future husband. Sometimes at weddings a common flat cake is prepared, into which a ring and a sixpence have been placed. When the company are about to disperse the cake is served round among the unmarried. She who gets the ring will shortly be married, but the finder of the sixpence is doomed to a single life.

The first egg laid by a hen is the object of the following superstition:—If it be broken into a tumbler of water over night, by the morning the white will tell the fair sorceress the trade of her future husband. If its shape resemble in some way a pair of scissors, he will be a tailor; if a boot or shoe, he will be a shoemaker, etc., etc. Sometimes a hole is made in the middle of four crossways and the ear applied to it; if the coming husband be a carpenter, the sound of sawing will be heard; if a shoe-maker, the tap, tap of his hammer, etc., etc.

. . . Stumbling upstairs, or seeing three crows sitting in the road, or dreaming of the dead, are accounted "signs of an approaching marriage."

Ib. p. 110.

DANCING IN A HOG'S TROUGH.

The practice of the elder sisters dancing in a hog's trough in consequence of the youngest sister marrying before them, is known in several parts of the county. The Rev. Hugh Pigot ascertained that the custom was known at Hadleigh. A lad from Great Whelnetham mentioned such a custom whilst giving evidence before the Justices at Bury St. Edmund's; and a correspondent of the "East Anglian" says that he knew of a case in the neighbourhood of Eye, where the

I 2

hog's trough was danced to pieces.   It is considered the most correct thing to dance in green stockings.

"The New Suffolk Garland," p. 177.

[Mr. Redstone met with an instance of this custom at Sutton, near Woodbridge, within the last twenty years.]

Sou'wester.—The very useful, but very ugly, oil-skin head-gear, used by fishermen, and making their comely faces really look very like some of the flat fish they deal in.   No glossary was needed to tell what a sou'wester is, nor, probably, for the little superstition attached to it.   The sailor, arriving from the north seas at nightfall, may go to his home, where the wife is sitting alone, thinking or not of him : just opening the door wide enough, he pitches his sou'wester into the room.   The true good wife will run to the door at once, not minding the sou'wester.   "But this may be old wives' mardle," said he who told me.

Ed. FitzGerald.   "The East Anglian," or Notes and Queries, edited by S. Tymms, vol. iii, p. 356.

XIII.—MISCELLANEOUS CUSTOMS, PHRASES. Etc.

'Seal.'

In my memory the ordinary wish at parting was ' The seal of the day to you.' . . .   This seal meant the season or time of the day.   It seems to be identical with the latter part of the word 'haysel,' which is still in common use for the hay season.

"Some materials for the Hist. of Wherstead."   By F. B. Zincke.

Hay-*seal*, wheat-*seal*, barley-*seal*, are the respective seasons of mowing, or sowing those products of the earth. . . .   Of an idle dissipated fellow, we say that he "keeps bad *seals*"; of poachers, that they are "out at all *seals* of the night"; of a sober, regular, and industrious man, that he attends to his business "at all *seals*," or that he keeps "good *seals* and meals." Sir Thomas Browne spells it *sele*; but we seem to come nearer to the Saxon. A. S. *sœl*, opportunitas. Pegge's Supplement to Grose.

Forby. "Vocabulary of E. Anglia," vol. ii, p. 293.

"To give one the seal of the day," *i.e.*, to be commonly civil to him, but nothing more.

Ibid. vol. ii, p. 433.

A Gate-Post Man.

The following conversation took place between me and a neighbour last August (1876):—Said he, "I sold my pigs at the right time; they are down three or four shillings." "But," said I, "have you got the money?" "Ay, ay," was his reply, "I am a *gate-post man*." I asked him what he meant by a *gate-post man*, when he told me that they called a man a *gate-post man* when he took his money first.

Mr. Halliwell (Glossary, p. 393) has the following passage:— *Gate-post bargain*, when the money is laid on the gate-post before the stock leave the field.—North.

"A Suffolk Parson in Suffolk Notes and Queries,"
Ipswich Journal.

Strewing Chaff Before the Door.

Query.—Can any of your correspondents throw light upon the following incident, which took place within the last twenty years in Suffolk?

Neighbours had good reason to believe that a man was in the habit of beating his wife, and otherwise ill-using her. To mark their sense of his conduct *they strewed chaff before his door.*—P.Q.

Answer.—It is obviously intended by "scattering *chaff* before a man's door" to intimate he has recently been *thrashing* (?).

"Suffolk Notes and Queries," Ipswich Journal.

'EARNEST.'

Earnest.—A sum given by a master on hiring a servant. A shilling is the usual sum. It is still a notion that if *Earnest* be not given and taken, it is not a complete hiring. . . . We usually pronounce it *arnest*.

Ed. Moor. "Suffolk Words and Phrases," p. 117.

'HANDSEL.'

Handsel.—First wearing a new coat, gown, or anything else, is *hanselling* it. It is extensively used, and always in a sense of first using—or initiatory—the first coin taken in the day by a pedlar or shop-keeper, is *hansel*. It is also used as a verb.

Ibid. p. 162.

Pay the Pepperidge.—A school-boy having on a new suit of clothes is subject to have a button pulled off unless he " pays the pepperidge " by giving a douceur to his fellows.

Ibid. p. 268.

SHEWEN THE COWT.

Shoeing the Colt.—A quaint phrase for the social exaction of a fine, on the introduction of an associate to any new office. If he meets his companions at a periodical dinner, a bottle of wine or a bowl of punch, in a certain rank of life, is a common fine on the *Colt's* health being drank. " Pahen his footen " is an equivalent phrase.

Ibid. p. 343.

FORFEITS.

Forfeits, s. pl. Shakespeare, in Measure for Measure, mentions "*forfeits* in a barber's shop." They exist to this day in some, perhaps in many, village shops. They are penalties for handling the razors, etc., offences very likely to be committed by lounging clowns, waiting for their turn to be scraped on a Saturday night, or Sunday morning. They are still, as of old, "more in mock

than mark." Certainly more mischief might be done 200 years
ago when the barber was also a surgeon. We have also *forfeits*
in every inn yard, payable in beer, by those who dabble in the
water cistern, carry candles into the stables, etc.

Forby. "Vocab. of E. Anglia," vol. i, p.

The 'Boy-Bishop.'

Strype says [Eccl. Mem., vol. iii, 310] that in 1556, "On St.
Nicolas Even, Saint Nicolas, that is a boy habited like a bishop
in pontificalibus went abroad singing after the old fashion, and was
received with many ignorant but well disposed people into their
houses, and had as much good cheer as ever was wont to be had
before." "To receive St. Nicholas' Clerks" is one of the points
mentioned by Foxe as essential to "a true faithful child of the
holy mother Church." It is by the same writer * related of
Argentine, Master of the Grammar School at Ipswich (A.D. 1556),
that "after the death of his wife, he was made a priest, taking
upon him divers times to preach, but never without his white
minever hood, such doctrine as was shameful to hear, saying mass,
and carrying about the pix in high processions : Furthermore,
leading the boy St. Nicholas with his minever hood about the
streets, for apples and belly-cheer : And whoso would not receive
him, he made them heretics, and such also as would not give his
faggot to the bonfire for Queen Mary's Child. And thus continued
he at Ipswich the most part of Queen Mary's days.

The "E. Anglian," or "Notes and Queries," new
series, vol. i, p. 171.

Pass, v. To "pass the bell" is to toll it for the purpose of
announcing a death. On the day of the funeral, the bell is not
said to be *passed*, but tolled or rung. The phrase alludes (with an
absurd misapplication of the word *pass*) to what was anciently
called the passing bell, otherwise the soul-peal, rung whilst the

---

* The Acts and Monuments of John Foxe, vol. viii, p. 282.—R.T.S.

sick lay in extremity, to admonish those who heard it to pray
for the soul while it was *passing*.

Forby. "Vocabulary of E. Anglia," vol. ii, p. 244.

WOODBRIDGE CHURCH BELLS.

In 1286 a violent storm raged upon the east coast of Suffolk,
destroying churches, houses, and much property. It was customary
to ring the bells to frighten away the demons of the storm, but in
this year the bells were out of repair, and so the Spirits of the
Air prevailed. Prior Thomas therefore caused great strife and
contention between the tenants of Roger Bygood (lord of the Manor
and proprietor of the Church) and the inmates of the Priory, by
demanding a fixed sum for the reparation of the bells. Riots
occurred, and to restore peace and order among those over whom
he acted as steward, Prior Thomas agreed with the tenants that a
sum of five shillings in silver would satisfy his demands. The
money was paid, but with this additional clause to the agreement,
that the said tenants were not bound to pay more to the repairs of
the fabric of the church and the restoration of the churchyard than
were other parishioners. . . . I would draw the attention of Wood-
bridgians to the fact that one good custom of bell-ringing has
dropped, the five a.m. bell to rouse man to his work, and that the
"Ave Bell," which rings just prior to divine service on Sundays,
is older than the Curfew, which I hope may never fail to be rung,
as it regulates the far distant clocks of

Yours truly, Antiquary.

(From a letter in the "Woodbridge Reporter," 1892.)

BELL-RINGERS' CUSTOMS.

I have in my possession a brown-glazed pot with handle, holding
about two gallons, and inscribed in rude letters arranged in four
lines :—

> " Here yov may see what
> I reqvst of Hanst (honest) Gentlmen
> My Baly (belly) filed of the bast I com
> Bvt now and then. 1716."

It was called the "Ringer's Pot," and was formerly carried from
house to house by the bell-ringers of Ixworth, in Suffolk, to receive
whatever beer the liberal parishioners might be disposed to bestow.
It has been disused about thirty years. It was probably made at
the celebrated pottery in the neighbouring parish of Wattisfield.—
J. Warren. *Ixworth.*

"E. Anglian," edited by S. Tymms, vol. i, p. 61.

HAWSTED CHURCH.

. . . The font . . . is of plain stone . . . having a hole at the
bottom. Through this hole the consecrated water, when it was to
be renewed, was let off, and descended to a cavity below, where
it was absorbed by the earth, that it might not be irreverently
thrown away, or applied to any profane or superstitious use. At
the upper edge of it are the remains of the iron fastenings, by
which the cover was formerly locked down, for fear of Sorcery.
How long this custom continued I cannot say, but a lock was
bought for the font in Brockdish church, in Norfolk, as late as
1553.

Sir J. Cullum. "Hist. and Antiq. of Hawsted."

Mr. Redstone sends the two interesting extracts that follow :—

On removing the floor in the Tower (1879), the foundation of the
wall of the West end of the Church was discovered, running in a
straight line from North to South, and near it was dug up a quantity
of animal bones, apparently those of a boar.

Dallinger's Church Record of Woodbridge, p. 83.

It was the custom in ancient times to bury a dog or a boar
alive under the corner-stone of a Church, that its ghost might
haunt the churchyard and drive off any who would profane it, *i.e.*,
witches or warlocks.

Henderson's "Folk-Lore," p. 238.

Within living memory the church of Raydon St. Mary, Suffolk, was decorated with birch* boughs on Whitsun day. . . .

BEATING THE BOUNDARIES.

Little Cornard Parish Accounts.

. . . There are several accounts extant for this same year, 1733. . . . Among the other items are " Laied out when we went a gangin £0 10s. 0d." . . . Going a ganging means " beating the bounds," a relic of the old processional Litanies in Rogation week.

> Cecil Deedes.   Wickham St. Paul's Rectory, Halstead.
> The " E. Anglian," or " Notes and Queries," new series, vol. iii, p. 73.

Extracts from the Churchwarden's Books of St. Clements, Ipswich.

1627. Payd the boyes when we went of perambellation, £00 09s. 00d.

1628. For bread and beare at Goodie Coulls uppon the perambulation daie for the boyes, £00 09s. 00d.

> The " E. Anglian " (new series), vol. iii, p. 356.

1638. Item ffor bread and beare giuen to the boyes when they wente the boundes of the parishe, £00 12s. 00d.

> *Ibid.* vol. iv, p. 5.

Bump. . . . At stated periods it is usual for parish-officers, attended by many idly-disposed boys and men, to go *a-bounding*, that is along (and to notice and mark) the bounds of the parish. This useful circumambulation is in some cases annual, in others

---

* Herrick, in his list of evergreen suitable at particular seasons for the decoration of houses, says :—

> " When Yew is out, then Birch comes in,
>   And many flowers beside,
>   Both of a fresh and fragrant Kinne,
>   To honour Whitsontide."

> H. A. W.   The " E. Anglian," or " Notes and Queries," new series, vol. iii, p. 197.

biennial, triennial, etc. And at its extremities, where a marked tree has generally been trained up, boys are soundly *bumped*, to impress on their memories, etc., the terminal fact. A stranger passing at the time, without a due consideration on the part of the bounders of who he may be, runs an imminent risk of having similar *impressions* made on his mind, etc.—for it is a sort of Saturnalia; a little drink being, perhaps, allowably charged in the parish accounts, superadded to the social collections of the *bounders* and *bumpers*, and sometimes even of a good humoured *bumpee*.

"Suffolk Words and Phrases," by Ed. Moor, p. 54.

HAWSTED.

Upon the bounds to the South-west grew some years ago a majestic tree called the *Gospel Oak*; it stood on an eminence and commanded an extensive prospect. Under the shade of this tree, the clergyman and his parishioners used to stop in their annual perambulations, and surveying a considerable extent of a fruitful and well-cultivated country, repeat some prayers of the Gospel only, proper for the occasion.

Sir J. Cullum's "History and Antiquities of Hawsted."

Oct. 31, 1777.—Last Saturday being the Anniversary of St. Crispin, the shoemakers made a grande Procession, on Horseback, from the Southgate, thro' all the Principal Streets, wth Trumpets in front and the rest of the band, joined wth drums, fifes, etc., between the divisions; on wch occasion there was more company in town than was ever remembered before. The Prince was mounted on a fine grey horse, and most magnificently habited: He was attended by his nobles superbly dress'd in green, and white, and his guards in blue and white: which made a very good appearance. His noble and warlike B^{r} Crispianus, appeared in a coat of mail, attended by his troops, in two divisions, one in red and white, the other in purple and white. They all rode in half-boots made of morocco in different colours adapted to their uniforms; their jackets and caps were extremely neat,

and in elegant taste, made all of leather. . . . The Prince
attended by his guard, with his torch bearers, and a grand band
of musick, playing before him, went to the play, and was rec^d
wth every mark of respect.

"The E. A.," ed. by S. Tymms, vol. i, p. 31.

Processions in honour of Bishop Blaize used to be held in Hadleigh,
on Feb. 3, within the memory of persons still living. Persons connected with the wool trade used to parade the town, and a female,
attired as shepherdess, rode in state in a post-chaise, carrying a
lamb in her lap. The custom has died away, but we have one
memorial of it in an old woman, who bears the Christian name
of "Shepherdess" from having been baptized soon after one of
these processions.—Hugh Pigot.

Ibid. p. 48.

In a contemporary common place book in MS. I find the
following notices of the celebration of St. Blaze's and St. Crispin's
days in Bury St. Edmunds.

February 3, 1777.—This day, Munday, being the anniversary
of Bishop Blaze, the same was observed in this town, in a manner
far surpassing anything of the kind ever seen. The Cavalcade
consisting of between 2 and 300 Woolcombers, upon Horses in
uniforms, properly decorated. Bishop Blaze, Jason, Castor and
Pollux, a band of musick, drums, colours, and everything necessary
to render the procession suitable to the greatness of the Woollen
Manufactory. The following lines were spoken by the Orators:—

"W^th boundless gratitude, Illustrious Blaze,
Again we celebrate, and speak thy Praise," etc.

Foy, s., a supper given by the owners of a fishing vessel at
Yarmouth, to the crew in the beginning of the season. It is
otherwise called a *bending-foy*, from the bending of the sails or
nets, as a ratification of the bargain. It must be from Fr. *foi*.

Forby. "Vocabulary of E. Anglia," vol. i, p. 121.

Hunting Squirrels on Christmas Day.—In many parts of the
country, particularly where there is much wood, the custom still

prevails of hunting squirrels on this day. . . . On Christmas morning half the idle fellows and boys in a parish assemble in any wood, or plantation, where squirrels are known to harbour; and having started their game, pursue it with sticks and stones from tree to tree, hallooing and shouting with all their might, till the squirrel is killed. . . . From the general discouragement shewn to this sport, probably comes the common saying, "Hunt Squirrels and make no noise."

Ibid. vol. ii, p. 420.

Kitty-witch, s.—1. A small species of cancer on our coast. . . . 2. A species of sea-fowl; probably more than one; certainly including that which is called by Pennant the *Kitty-wake.* 3. A female spectre; arrayed in white, of course. The plumage of sea-birds contains, in almost all instances, a large proportion of pure and brilliant white. 4. A woman dressed in a grotesque and frightful manner; otherwise called a *kitch-witch,* probably for the sake of a jingle. It was customary, many years ago at Yarmouth, for women of the lowest order to go in troups from house to house to levy contributions, at some season of the year, and on some pretence, which nobody now seems to recollect, having men's shirts over their own apparel, and their faces smeared with blood. These hideous beldames have long discontinued their perambulations; but in memory of them, one of the many rows in that town is called Kitty-witch row.

Ibid. vol. ii, p. 186.

Devil Worship.—Rendlesham, or Rendilisham, *i.e.,* as Bede interprets it, the House of Rendilus. . . . . Cambden tells us, "Redwald, King of the East-Angles, commonly kept his Court here; he was the first of all that people who was baptized, and received Christianity: but afterwards, being seduced by his wife, he had (as *Bede* expresses it) in the self-same Church, one Altar for the Religion of Christ, and another little Altar for the Sacrifices of Devils." . . . .

"The Suffolk Traveller," first published by Mr. John
Kirby. 2nd Edition, London, printed for J. Shave,
at the Stationer's Arms, in the Butter Market.
MDCCLXIX.

MARRIAGE CUSTOMS IN SUFFOLK.

There is a . . . Scotch proverb, "It is better to marry over the midden than over the moor." . . . I am not aware of the existence of any proverb to this effect in East Anglia; but the usual practice of the working classes is in strict accordance with it.   Whole parishes have intermarried to such an extent that almost everybody is related to, or connected with, everybody else. . . .

"Marry in Lent,
And you'll live to repent."

"To change the name, and not the letter,
Is a change for the worst, and not for the better."

i.e. it is unlucky to marry a man whose surname begins with the same letter as her own.

. . . The attendance at the wedding of agricultural labourers is naturally small; but it is very remarkable that neither father nor mother of bride or bridegroom come with them to church. I can hardly recollect more than one instance of any of the parents being present at the ceremony, and then what brought the bridegroom's father was the circumstance of the ring having been left behind. . . . The usual attendants at a labourer's wedding are only three—the official father, the bridesmaid, and the groomsman; the two latter being, if possible, an engaged couple, who purpose to be the next pair to come up to the altar. . . .

The parties very frequently object to sign their names, and try to get off from doing so, even when they can write very fairly, preferring to set their *mark* to the entry in the register.

Suffolk.   C. W. J., "The Book of Days," edited
by R. Chambers, vol. i, p. 722.

"They that wive
Between sickle and scythe
Shall never thrive."

J. T. Varden, "E. A. Handbook," p. 110.

Ring-finger.—As elsewhere, the third finger of the left hand. We have a persuasion that this finger was thus selected, because

an artery comes direct to it from the heart—a distinction enjoyed
by no other digit.

Ed. Moor. "Suffolk Words and Phrases," p. 295.

THE PLOUGHMAN'S FEASTING DAYS.

"This would not be slipt,
Old guise must be kept.
Good housewives, whom God has enriched enough,
Forget not the feasts, that belong to the plough:
The meaning is only to joy and be glad,
For comfort, with labour, is fit to be had."

Plough Monday. *

"Plough Monday, next after that Twelfthtide is past,
Bids out with the plough, the worst husband is last,
If ploughman get hatchet, or whip to the screen,
Maids loseth their cock, if no water be seen."

Shrovetide.

"At Shrovetide to shroving, go thresh the fat hen,
If blindfold can kill her, then give it thy men.
Maids, fritters and pancakes enow see ye make,
Let slut have one pancake for company sake."

Sheep-Shearing.

"Wife, make us a dinner, spare flesh, neither corn,
Make wafers and cakes, for our sheep must be shorn,
At sheep-shearing, neighbours none other thing crave,
But good cheer and welcome, like neighbours to have."

The Wake-Day. †

"Fill oven with flawns, Jenny, pass not for sleep,
Tomorrow, thy father his wake-day will keep.
Then every wanton may dance at her will,
Both Tomkin with Tomlin, and Jenkin with Gill."

* . . . The men and maid servants strove to outvie each other in early rising
on Plough Monday. If the ploughman could get any of the implements of his
vocation by the fireside before the maid could put on her kettle, she forfeited her
Shrovetide cock. The evening concluded with a good supper.

† On the night preceding the day of the dedication of the parish church, which is
always identified with some Saint in the Romish Calendar at least, the young
parishioners used to watch in the church till morning, and to feast the next day.
This practice was likely to lead to irregularities, and was properly changed to waking
at the oven in each particular house.

Harvest-Home. *

"For all this good feasting, yet art thou not loose,
Till ploughman thou givest his harvest-home goose.
Though goose go in stubble, I pass not for that,
Let goose have a goose, be she lean, be she fat."

Seed-Cake.

"Wife, some time this week, if the weather hold clear,
An end of wheat sowing we make for this year:
Remember thou therefore, though I do it not,
The seed-cake, the pasties, and furminty pot."

Twice a-week Roast.

"Good plowmen, look weekly, of custom and right,
For roast meat on Sundays, and Thursdays at night.
Thus doing and keeping such custom and guise,
They call thee good huswife, they love thee likewise."

Threshing the Hen.—This singular custom is almost obsolete, yet it certainly is practised, even now, in at least one obscure part of the kingdom. . . . .

"At Shrovetide to shroving, go thrash the fat hen,
If blindfold can kill her, then give it thy men.
Maids, fritters and pancakes enough see you make,
Let slut have one pancake, for company sake."

So directs Tusser in his " Five Hundred Points of Good Husbandry, 1620." 4ᵗᵒ. On this his annotator, " Tusser Redivivus, 1710," (8ᵛᵒ. June, p. 15) annexes an account of the custom. "The hen is hung at a fellow's back, who has also some horse-bells about him; the rest of the fellows are blinded, and have boughs in their hands, with which they chase this fellow and his hen about some large court or small enclosure. The fellow with his hen and bells shifting as well as he can, they follow the sound, and sometimes hit him and his hen, other times, if he can get behind one of them, they thresh one another well favour'dly; but the jest is, the maids are to blind the fellows, which they do with their aprons, and the cunning baggages will

* It appears that a goose used formerly to be given, at harvest-home, to those who had not overturned a load of corn, in carrying, during harvest.—Tusser's " Five Hundred Points of Good Husbandry," p. 270.

endear their sweethearts with a peeping-hole, whilst the others look out as sharp to hinder it. After this the hen is boil'd with bacon, and store of pancakes and fritters are made."

Tusser's annotator, "Redivivus," adds, after the hen-thrashing: " She that is noted for lying a-bed long, or any other miscarriage, hath the first pancake presented to her, which most commonly falls to the dog's share at last, 'for no one will own it their due." . . . . Old Tusser himself, by a reference, denotes that this was a sport in Essex and Suffolk.

> "The Every Day Book," by William Hone. London : printed for Thomas Tegg, 73, Cheapside. (1826.) p. 246.

Pancake-Day, s. Shrove Tuesday.—Ill-luck betides the family in which *pancakes* are not served up on that day.

> Forby. "Vocab. of E. Anglia," vol. ii, p. 242.

Customary Viands for particular Days.—On certain days in the year it was the custom of old times to prepare a particular kind of food, which was considered peculiar to that day. Some of these customs are still in use amongst us. On Michaelmas Day, for instance, every person, who can afford it, has a roast goose for dinner. Christmas is a season of festivity in all parts of the kingdom; but in Suffolk, and particularly in High Suffolk, that festival is begun in a way which is, perhaps, not general in other parts. On the morning of Christmas Day, in many farmhouses, a large quantity of frumenty is prepared, and the labourers on the farm, with their wives and children, are invited to breakfast upon it. It is considered a great treat, and is really a most nourishing and delicious food. . . . In Suffolk [on Christmas Eve] hot elderberry wine, with spice, is the usual regale for holiday friends. On Shrove Tuesday, pancakes are indispensable; but the " fat hen " is never now threshed ; nor, indeed, is there any tradition of that barbarous sport having been practised in these counties for many years. . . . In Suffolk we have no particular

dish at Easter, but Whit Sunday is always celebrated with baked
custards, and if possible, with gooseberry pies; and these delicacies
are standing dishes during the whole of Whitsuntide.

Ibid. vol. ii, p. 422.

Kichel.*—A flat Christmas cake, of a triangular shape, with sugar
and a few currants *strowd* over the top—differing, only in shape,
I believe, from a *bun.* Cocker says, "*Kichel* is Saxon—a kind
of cake or God's *Kichel,* a cake given to God-children when they
ask blessing of their God-father."

Ed. Moor. "Suffolk Words and Phrases," p. 192.

Soham Fair Bread.—A loaf made of new wheat.

Mr. Redstone, Woodbridge.

Groaning-Cake.—A cake made on such occasions [*i.e.* lying-in],
with which about as many superstitious tricks are played as with
bride-cake.

Forby, vol. ii, p. 142.

Hot Cross Buns.—Hot cross buns, if properly made, will never
get mouldy. To make them properly, you must do the whole
of the business on the Good Friday itself; the materials must be
mixed, the dough made, and the buns baked on that day, and
this, I think, before a certain hour; but whether this hour is
sunrise or church-time I cannot say.

Suffolk. C. W. J., "Book of Days," vol. ii, p. 323.

Tusser in his "Five Hundred points of Husbandry," says:

"Yer Christmas be passed, *let Horses be lett blood,*
For many a purpose it doth him much good:
The day of St. Steven,† old fathers did use,
If that do mislike thee some other day chuse."

W. Hone. "The Every Day Book," vol. i, p. 1644.

---

* cf. Aubrey, "Remaines of Gentilisme and Judaisime," p. 7. (F. L. Socy., 1881.)
† Hone refers to "Naorgeorgus," translated by Barnaby Googe.

"Then followeth Saint Stephen's day, whereon doth every man
His horses jaunt a course abrode, as swiftly as he can,
Until they doe extreemely sweate, and than they let them blood,
For this being done upon this day, they say doth do them good,
And keepes them from all maladies and sickness through the yeare,
As if that Steven any time took charge of horses heare."

May Day.—It was an old custom in Suffolk, in most farm-houses, that any servant, who could bring in a branch of hawthorn in full blossom on the first of May, was entitled to a dish of cream for breakfast. This custom is now disused, not so much from the reluctance of the masters to give the reward, as from the inability of the servants to find the white-thorn in flower. The alteration of the style will go some way to account for it, but scarcely far enough. It very seldom happens that any blossoms are seen open even on Old May Day.

Forby, vol. ii, p. 426.

"This is the day,
And here is our May,
The finest ever seen,
It is fit for the queen;
So pray, ma'm, give me a cup of your cream."

J. P. Varden.   "E. A Handbook," p. 125.

Gloves at Lammas (Aug. 1st).—It was once customary in England .... to give money to servants on Lammas-day, to buy gloves, hence the term *Glove Silver*. It is mentioned among the ancient customs of the Abbey of St. Edmund's, in which the clerk of the cellarer had 2d., the cellarer's squire 11d., and the cowherd a penny. . . . .

Hampson's Medii Ævi Kalendarium, quoted in " Book of Days," vol. ii, p. 154.

[From " *The titles containing the expences of household and other forren charges and money defraied by me, Thomas Fryer, for the use of my m*r. *Thomas Kytson Squire, beginning the first of October*, 1572.]

December.

Payed for iij sheets thick grose paper to decke the bores * heade in Christmas xij*d*.

* At Christmas the entry of the boar's head, decked with laurel and rosemary recalled the sacrifice of the boar to Frigga at the midwinter feast of old heathendom —J. R. Green's " Conquest of England." London: Macmillan & Co., 1883, p. 11

More payd to Bushe of Bury, paynter, for the paynting the bores heade with sondry colors ij^s.

To Meg and Mary to play at maw in Christmas time, x^s.

In reward to Stephen, Mr. Longe's man, for playing an interlude before my m^r. in Chrystmas, xx^s.

May.

[In London.] For green boughs, ij^d. (Probably to adorn the house at the pastime of the midsummer watch.)

June.

[In London.] For the hire of a man on Midsomer^n night with a coralet to attend upon my Lord Mayor, iiij^s.

(A minute description of the pastime called the Midsummer Watch will be found in Stowe's survey of London, p. 159, Lond. 1603. In a household book at Hengrave of the Lady Long, for the year 1546, the following entry occurs :—P^d to xxx men for weying cf yor La harneys on Midsommer Eve and S^t. Peter's Eve, y^t is to cay x^s. to my L. Mayor, and xx^s. to Sir Roland Hill." Thus it would appear that it was the custom to enter the houses of individuals, in the city, for the purpose of examining the state of their arms, a practice Stowe does not directly notice, though he speaks particularly of the commodities of the pastime.)

January.

For a bull to kill in Christmas time, xxxiiij^s, iiij^d.

In rewarde to Richard Reede, one of the wayghts of Cambridge, for his attendance in Christmas time, xx^s.

Gage's Hengrave, p. 198.

Roarers.—The men who shovel out the herrings f^r the lugger into the ped, or f^r the ped along the fish-curing floor, with *roaring shovels*. This reminds me of a song once current on y^r coast, of w^h I can lay hold of no more than the burden, I suppose. It was told me by a clergyman.

> "The roaring boys of Pakefield
> Didn't know what to contrive,
> They had but one poor parson,
> And him they buried alive."

Edward FitzGerald's Works, vol. ii, p. 466.

(Alternative Version.)

"The roaring boys of Pakefield,
Oh how they all do thrive !
They had but one poor parson,
And him they buried alive."

(Propi Septuagenarius.) " Suffolk Notes and Queries,"
Ipswich Journal.

[See Brand on " Roaring Boyes," in " Drinking Customs," Pop
Antiq., vol. ii, p. 203.]

Supernaculum.—A word well known and occasionally heard in
social circles in Suffolk—generally understood to mean little else
than an excellent bottle—something supercurious. Few of us, I
ween, were aware of its origin, which Nares shews in a very
curious article. . . . It is a kind of mock Latin, intending to mean
on the nail, and is thus explained in a quotation from Pierce
Pennelesses.

Drinking super nagulum ; a devise of drinking, new come out or
Fraunce, which is, after a man hath turned up the bottom of the cup,
to drop it *on his nails,* and to make a pearle with that is left ; which
if it slide, and he cannot make it stand on, by reason ther's too much,
he must drink again for his pennance. . . .—Gay's Fest. Notes, p. 102.

Ed. Moor. " Suffolk Words and Phrases," p. 409.

[See Brand's Pop. Antiq., vol. ii, p. 202, p. 209.]

Owd Shue.—An old shoe ; which I introduce for the purpose of
noticing that we still retain the phrase of " throwing an *owd shue*
aater one " for good luck.

Ed. Moor. " Suffolk Words and Phrases," p. 263.

" Ah, deeow, hull an owd shew aater me for good luck."
Ibid. p. 343.

Silly Suffolk (Vol. i, p. 197, etc.).—An instance of the peculiar
use of the word " silly " as pointed out in previous numbers of the
" East Anglian," is seen in one of the inscriptions in the last number

(p. 288)—"*this syllie shrine.*" *   A certain parish in the County is known as *Silly Hemingstone*; amongst its neighbours are *Proud Coddenham*, *Lousy Barham*, *Worm-eaten Gosbeck*, and *Plum-pudding Ashbocking*.

> G. M. L.   The "East Anglian," or "Notes and Queries," new series, vol. ii, p. 303.

Eastern Sunday. . . . It may not be impertinent, though not exactly apposite, to remark here, that the female baptismal name, *Esther* or *Hester* (by no means an uncommon one) is always pronounced *Easter;* no doubt the name of the Saxon goddess, handed down without interruption or change, and confounded with that of the Persian Queen.

> Forby.   "Vocab. of E. Anglia," vol. i, p. 104.

Bess o' Bedlam, s. a sort of vagrant very common in this country thirty or forty years ago; but now very nearly, if not quite, extinct. . . . . They were wont to announce themselves as inmates of Bedlam, allowed in some lucid interval to range the country, and return at a stated time to their confinement.   They talked in a wild incoherent manner, were great annoyances to everybody, objects of great terror to many, and, from the general wish to be rid of them as soon as possible, were likely to collect considerable contributions.   They were in existence in Shakespeare's time, who speaks of "Bedlam beggars with their roaring voices."   The name is not yet obsolete. Any female maniac, or any whose dress, manners, and language, are wild, disorderly, and incoherent, is still called a *Bess o' Bedlam.*— V. Tom o' Bedlam.

> *Ibid.* vol. i, p. 23.

Wolf, s.—1. A preternatural or excessive craving for food.   "Surely he must have a wolf in his stomach."   2. A gnawing internal pain, proceeding from cancer or other ulcer, which, as a ravenous beast,

---

* "Iohn Browne of Waltone Gentleman Philip Browns sone & heir
Brother unto Winifred his onlie sister deare
Foreseeinge that mans life is fraile & subject vnto death
Hath chosen this syllie shrine, to shrevd his corps in earth." . . etc.
Inscription in Church of St. John de Sepulchre, Norwich.

preys on the intestines. A poor woman, whose husband had long been thus afflicted, and who had, with much difficulty, been prevailed upon to allow his body to be opened, told the author that the Doctors had found *the wolf*, and carried it away. Had she supposed it to be a morbid part of the body, she would certainly not have allowed this; but she believed, *bonâ fide*, that it was a voracious animal, which had somehow found its way in, and had been detected, and turned out, too late.

Ibid. vol. ii, p. 378.

Wolf.—I can recollect certain women, oldish ones I think, who were generally believed—by boys and girls I mean—to have a wolf in their stomachs. The notion was encouraged by the women themselves, who, it may be imagined, more disposed to eat than to work, thus accounted for an inordinate appetite, and obtained commiseration and relief.

Ed. Moor. "Suffolk Words and Phrases," p. 490.

Composant.—Some years ago a young sailor was telling me of a "*composite*" lighting on each mast of a yawl during a stormy night. I didn't understand the word though I knew the meaning; an older sailor explained that "composant" was the proper word. I was not the wiser till I chanced upon the explanation in *Dampier's Voyages*. "After four o'clock the thunder and the rain abated, and then we saw a *corpus sant* at our maintopmast head, on the very top of the bruck of the spindle. This sight rejoiced our men exceedingly, for the height of the storm is commonly over when the *corpus sant* is seen aloft, but when they are seen lying on deck, it is generally accounted a bad sign." "A *corpus sant* is a certain small glittering light; when it appears, as this did, on the very top of the mainmast, or at a yard-arm, it is like a star; but when it appears on the deck it resembles a great glow-worm. The Spaniards have another name for it, though I take even this to be a Spanish or Portuguese name, and a corruption only of 'corpus sanctum' [I suppose *the host*, or starry pyx that holds it], and I have been told that when they see them they presently

go to prayers, and bless themselves for the happy sight. I have
heard some ignorant seamen discoursing how they have seen them
creep, or, as they say, travel, about in the scuppers, telling many
dismal stories that happened at such times. But I did never see
any one stir out of the place where it was first fixed, except
upon deck, where every sea washed it about; neither did I ever
see any but when we have had hard rain as well as wind; and
therefore do believe it is some jelly." . . . Dampier's men probably
called the word *corpusant* or *corposant*, whence *composant*, and,
after the invention of certain candles peculiar to the nineteenth
century, *composite*.

> Edward Fitzgerald. *Works*, vol. ii, p. 466, "Suffolk
> Sea Phrases" (Houghton, Mifflin, and Co.'s
> Edition), 1887.

Hobby-Lantern.—The jack-o'-lantern, will-o'-th'-wisp, etc., as
given by Forby. Nor should he (Jack I mean) need bringing in
here, but for a habit of his which I only lately heard of on the
coast—namely, Jack's inveterate hatred, or jealousy, (or love?) of
any light but his own. He will fly and dash at lighted windows,
I am told; and the sailor from whom I learned this, knew of a
friend, who, coming home at night with a lantern, was violently
assaulted in that quarter.

> *Ibid.* p. 466.

Joan's silver pin, s. a single article of finery, produced occasionally,
and ostentatiously among dirt and sluttery.

> "The Vocabulary of E. Anglia," by Rev. R. Forby,
> vol. ii, p. 175.

Kiss-me-at-the-Garden-Gate, s. a fanciful, yet rather a pretty,
name of the several beautiful varieties of the garden pansy.

> *Ibid.* p. 184.

Wood-sprite, s. the Woodpecker.

> *Ibid.* p. 378.

* *Tittle-my-fancy*, s. pansies. *Viola tricolor*, Lin.

Ibid. p. 350.

Old-witch, s. the cockchaffer, or midsummer dor, which, after sunset, on a fine evening in June or July, "wheels it's droning flight." . . .

Ibid. p. 238.

Shoes and Stockings, s. pl. The variety of primrose and polyanthus which has one flower sheathed within another.

Ibid. p. 297.

Devil's toe nails.—Gryhea incurvata.

Mr. Redstone.

Bird of the Eye, s. the pupil, or rather, perhaps, the little re-fracted image on the retina, or that of a very near spectator reflected from the cornea. In many languages there seems to be some delicate or endearing term of this kind. . . .

Forby, vol. i, p. 24.

Beggar's Velvet, s. the lightest particles of down shaken from a feather-bed, and left by a sluttish housemaid to collect under the bed till it covers the floor for want of due sweeping, and she gets a scolding from her dame.

Ibid. vol. i, p. 22.

. . . . I may mention a ludicrous Suffolk phrase descriptive of a person not quite so sharp as he might be : he is spoken of as "short of buttons," being, I suppose, considered an unfinished article.

Suffolk. C. W. J., "Book of Days," vol. ii, p. 322.

Bungay-play, s. a simple straightforward way of playing the game at whist, by leading cards in succession, without any plan to make the best of the hand. Perhaps it was applied before the invention of whist, to an unskilful manner of playing old games, as primero, gleek,

---

* Tittle, v. to tickle. A. S. Kittelan titillare.—Forby, vol. ii, p. 350.

etc. At any rate we are not to understand that, in this name, an indiscriminate, and therefore an unjust, censure is cast upon all the good people of Bungay for their unskilfulness. In O.E. *bungar* was synonymous with *bungler*.

Forby, vol. i, p. 46.

To sit where the Dog was hanged.—It means a succession of petty mischances. The good woman breaks her thread, drops her stitches, overturns her snuff-box, scalds her fingers with her tea-kettle; or if she sits down to play soberly at cribbage, trickets, or all-fours, she meets with all the modes of ill-luck attendant on any of those games. And, after sustaining a competent number of these "miseries of human life," accounts for them by exclaiming, "Surely I sit where the dog was hanged!"

Ibid. vol. ii, p. 409.

In the "Gentleman's Magazine" for November, 1783—selec. i, 362 —are some translations from a scarce book entitled, "Corolla Varia, by the Rev. W. Hawkins, Schoolmaster of *Hadleigh*, *Suffolk*,"— printed at Cambridge, 1634. The translations are of three authentic registers of the Monastery of *St. Edmundsbury*. One runs thus:— "This Indenture certifies that Master John Swassham, sacrist, with the consent of the prior and convent, demise and let to ——, the manor called *Habyrdon* in *Bury* —, and the said ——, his executors, etc., shall find or cause to be found *one white bull* every year of his term, so often as it shall happen that any gentlewoman (*mulierem generosum*), or any other woman, from devotion or vows by them made, shall visit the tomb of the glorious martyr St. Edmund, to make the oblation of the said white bull, etc. Dated the 4th of June, in the second year of King Henry VII." (A.D. 1487). The other indentures, nearly similar, are of the 11th and 25th of Henry VIII.

The following are from Mr. Hawkins's observations thereon. . . .

" Whenever a married woman wished to be pregnant, this white bull, who enjoyed full ease and plenty in the fields of *Habyrdon*, never meanly yoked to the plough, nor ever cruelly baited at the stake, was led in procession through the principal streets of the

town to the principal gate of the monastery, attended by all the
monks singing, and a shouting crowd; the woman walking by him
and stroking his milk-white sides and pendent dewlaps. The bull
being then dismissed, the woman entered the church, and paid her
vows at the altar of St. Edmund, *kissing the stone*, and entreating
with tears the blessing of a child."

. . . Of the above-named manor of *Habyrdon* are probably those
deep indented meadows now called *Haberden*, close to the town,
on the right as you enter *Bury* from *Ipswich*: they still appertain
to the guild—derived, uninterruptedly perhaps, from the better days
of the monastery which covered them.

Ed. Moor. "Oriental Fragments," p. 518. 1834.

CHEVINGTON.

In the time of Abbot Cratfield. . . . the customs were particularly
defined. Among the free tenants, *liberi tenentes*, was Philip de
Kedynton. . . . He was to do one ploughing, *arrura*, at the time
of sowing at the *Plough-ale*, and to find a reaper in autumn for
one day at the *Alebene*. William Redenhale, another customary
tenant, was to do work at the Plough-ale, and Alebene; and
also to do three ploughings at the *Lovebene*.

J. Gage. "Hist. and Antiq. of Suffolk," p. 324.

St. Valentine's Day.—In this part of the county of Suffolk,
Valentine's Day appears to be the great gift day of the year;
and the many costly tokens of affection appear to be accompanied
by as much mystery and fun as on New Year's Day in Paris. . .
H. *Lowestoft.*

"The East Anglian," vol. i, p. 24.

Hunting the wren on Valentine's Day is not entirely out of use.

Gage's "Hist. and Antiq. of Suffolk." Thingoe
Hundred. Foot-note, p. xxvii.

Feet traced on Leaden Roofs. — When Sir Symonds D'Ewes of
Stowlangtoft, Suffolk, in 1627, was on his wedding tour, he says

" Wee went both up to the topp of King's Colledge Chapell [Oxford] on the north side whereoff upon the leades my wives foote was sett, *being one of the least in England,* her age and stature considered, and *her arms exsculped within the compasse of the foote in a small escocheon.*" (Notes to Hearne's Lib. Niger Scaccarii, p. 644.) . . . That the practice of " setting the foot " was common every leaden roof will tell us, and that it was not confined to "rude and ignorant people," the following extract from Stowe's *Chronicle,* as well as the above note of Sir Symonds D'Ewes, will curiously show:—" 1606. And then the King [of Denmark] and the Lord Chamberlayne, with others, ascended the top of the steeple [at Westminster Abbey] and when he had surveied the cittie, he held his foote still whilst Edward Soper, Keper of the Steple, with his knife cut the length and breadth thereof in the lead, and for a lasting remembrance thereof the said Soper within a few days after made the King's character [*i.e.* his name and title] in gild copper, and fixed it in the middest of the print of the King's foote. . . ."

L. " The E. Anglian," vol. iv, p. 192.

Manor.—I did not at first understand what was meant by a ship "wreckt upon the Manor." What did that mean? Why, stranded above the ebb, to which the Lord of the Manor's right extends. And if the vessel not only strikes, but go to pieces there, he claims a fee from the owner. Think of that last drop in the cup! To be wreckt, half-drown'd oneself, and one's ship quite lost, and then to have to pay a fee for the privilege of her knocking to pieces where she lies!

Ed. FitzGerald. *Ibid.* vol. iv, p. 113.

EAST ANGLIAN PILGRIMAGES.

The will of William Crispe, shoemaker, of Bury, 1516, mentions "Our Lady of Grace in Ippiswiche," and " Our Lady of Walsyngham" (Bury Registry, Lib. Hood, p. 38) as places of pilgrimage. At this time the Ipswich lady had attained her highest repute, having just worked a miraculous cure in the presence of the Abbot of Bury, on the daughter of a Sir Roger Wentford, of Essex, a young lady of sixteen, "who was many wayes vexed and troubled with the deville's appearing to her, so that she had utterly forgotten God and all his workes." This famous image was ignominiously burnt in Smithfield, in twenty years after this occurrence.—Hollingsworth's *Hist. of Stowmarket*, p. 106.

The will of Alice Cosyn, of Farnham, Suffolk, 1524, enumerates several other places of great sanctity in the East Anglian district—" I will that Walter Noble go on pilgrimage to oure blessed ladye of huntington, to oure blissed ladye of redychame, to Busshop Alcocke, and to Sainte Awdrie. It'm, I will that Richarde Noble go on pilgramage to oure blissed ladie of Wulpette, and to our blissed ladie of grace."

Pilgrim. "E. Anglian," vol ii, p. 226.

Spit in both hands.—For a good bargain.

Weep.—The nails weeping with rust is one sign of the ship's complaining.

Gay-gown Day.—"What the likes of us sometimes say in fine weather at sea; thinkin', I suppose, of the women ashore."

Ed. Fitzgerald. "East Anglian," vol. iv, p. 262.

Grace.—" Laid up in Grace "; laid up " in lavender," away from common use.

Ibid. p. 111.

Renewed.—When a whole new piece of *lint* has been added to the old, nets are "renewed"; when the old lint is simply repaired, they are " *Bet ups.*" And good nets well bet up, and well renew'd, will *kill* themselves catching fish, they say, before wearing out.

Ibid. p. 263.

Butter a Cat's Paws.—Not a phrase but a fact; being a charm sometimes resorted to by the " ignorant " hereabout to attach a cat to a house, for which, as they gravely say, " She's a bringing up."

Company-Keepers.—Ships that sail together, as well as Lovers who "walk" together. "That old Jemima and Woilet (Violet) are rare company-keepers."

Gast-Cope.—(I know not how else to write it, nor how at all to account for it.) "Going gast cope" without hire, or pay, as a boy on his first voyage.

Ibid. vol. iv, p. 111.

Rattlin' Sam.—A term of endearment, I suppose, used by Salwagers for a nasty shoal off Corton coast.

Red Caps.—Formerly, I am told, the master-boat among the Luggers; she that had raised most money by the voyage, distinguished her crew with red caps, in token of victory.

Services.—Pieces of old lint, rope, spun yarn (always sounded *spunnion*, you know) wrapt round rope or warp to prevent its chafing. The word is not peculiar to these parts, but is noted here because among the Luggers, beer, biscuit, and cheese should, according to old usage, be handed round at this ceremony, which comes close on the voyage.

Ibid. vol. iv, p. 115.

XIV.—MISCELLANEOUS OMENS.

It is regarded as a bad omen, if when you leave a house you replace the chair on which you have been sitting against the wall; the probability, if not the certainty, in that case is that you will never visit that house again.

"The New Suffolk Garland," p. 179.

If you have your clothes mended upon your back you will be ill-spoken of.

Ibid. p. 180.

If you break two things, you will break a third. A lady saw one of her servants take up a coarse earthenware basin and deliberately throw it down upon the brick floor. "What *did* you do that for?"

asked the mistress. "Because, ma'am, I'd broke tew things," answered the servant; "so I thout the third 'd better be this here," pointing to the remains of the least valuable piece of pottery in the establishment, which had been sacrificed to glut the vengeance of the offended ceramic deities.

Ibid. p. 180.

I once had a servant who was very much given to breaking glass and crockery. . . . "Let her buy something," said the cook, "and that will change the luck." "Decidedly," said the mistress, "it will be as well that she should feel the inconvenience herself." "Oh I didn't mean that, ma'am," was the reply; "I meant that it would change the luck."

Suffolk. C. W. J., "Book of Days," vol. ii, p. 105.

Friday is considered an unlucky day. Sunday, on the other hand, is regarded as an auspicious day; and if persons have been ill and have become convalescent, they almost always get up for the first time on Sundays.

"The New Suffolk Garland," p. 179.

Amongst Suffolk people, to sneeze three times before breakfast is a pledge that you will soon have a present made to you. The sneezing of a cat. however, is considered to be an evil omen; it is a sign that the family of the owner will all have colds.

Ibid. p. 178.

To sleep in a room with the whitethorn bloom in it during the month of May will surely be followed by some great misfortune.

Choice Notes (vol. vii, p. 201).

Broom, Whitethorn.—Formerly I used to hear the rhymes:—

> "Sweep with a broom that is cut in May,
> And you will sweep the head of the house away."

. . . The somewhat similar superstition that you will die before the year is out if you bring May-flower into your house.

"Some Materials for the Hist. of Wherstead," by
F. B. Zincke, p. 179.

It is a common misbelief that an abundance of fruit on this plant (*i.e.* hawthorn) is an indication that the coming winter will be severe, because we have before us a providential store of food for many of the feathered tribe.

Ibid.

Kid.—To signify by hand and arm (A. S. cydan) how many herrings on board; the arm struck forward signifies a last; waved round, a thousand.

I forgot to mention under "clock-calm," that those potent, grave, and reverend seniors, the *old* eight-day clocks, are supposed to know a good deal of what goes on in the house they inhabit, more indeed than the masters themselves; fore-knowing, and by some hurried ticking or inward convulsion, foretelling the death of some member of the family. I was told of one distinctly "*kidding*" the approaching decease of his old mistress. "There was no mistake at all about it— why the old clock fared in the biggest of agony."

Edward Fitzgerald. *Works*, vol. ii, p. 466. "Suffolk Sea Phrases."

Thief in the Candle.—A defective wick, which not being equally consumed, causes the candle to gutter and waste. A coming *letter* is foretold by a projecting spark on the *snaste*. [snast, or sneest. The snuff of a candle or lamp.]

Ibid. p. 426.

Spilling the Salt.—This ominous accident is still felt in all its full force among us, but the threatened result may be in part averted by throwing a little of the spilled article over your left shoulder.

Thirteen at Table.—I have known and now know, persons in genteel life, who did, and do, not sit down to table unmoved with twelve others. And so far is this feeling carried that one of the thirteen is requested to dine at a side table! . . . Our notion is that one of

thirteen so partaking will die ere the expiring of the year. . . .
Hence also may have arisen the phrase of the devil's dozen. Thus
in Scottish "*Deil's dozen*," the number thirteen: apparently from
the idea that the thirteenth is the devil's lot. "Jamieson's Scottish
Dictionary," 8vo. Thirteen is likewise called a *baker's dozen.* In
vulgar eyes this tradesman is too often contemplated in connection
with the Devil.

Ibid. p. 384.

" *Gifts* " *on the nails.*—Small white specks on the nails are sure
indications that those who are so fortunate as to have them will
in some way or other be the better for them; though perhaps
not literally in the manner implied by the name. And some
sagacious old women are very shrewd in explaining, from their
number, size, position, etc., in what manner it will be; and
particularly in accounting for anything of the kind which has
really happened.

There is a superstition also respecting cutting the nails. . . .
To cut them on a Tuesday is thought particularly auspicious.
Indeed, if we are to believe an old rhyming saw on this subject,
every day of the week is endowed with it's several and peculiar
virtue, if the nails are invariably cut on that day and no other.
The lines are as follow :—

> " Cut them on Monday, you cut them for health ;
> Cut them on Tuesday, you cut them for wealth ;
> Cut them on Wednesday, you cut them for news ;
> Cut them on Thursday, a new pair of shoes ;
> Cut them on Friday, you cut them for sorrow ;
> Cut them on Saturday, see your true-love to-morrow ;
> Cut them on Sunday, the devil will be with you all the week."

Forby, vol. ii, p. 410.

" *Gifts* " *on Nails.*—The rhyme given below gives their mystic
significance, commencing with the thumb and going on to the little
finger :—

> " Gift—Friend—Foe—
> Sweetheart—journey to go."

There is another proverb which says :—

> " A gift on the thumb
> Is sure to come;
> A gift on the finger
> Is sure to linger."

J. T. Varden, "East Anglian Handbook," p. 107.

It is dangerous to let blood in the dog-days.

If a servant goes to his place by daylight, he will never stay long in it.

Wherever the wind lies on Ash Wednesday, it continues during the whole of Lent.

If you set the broom in a corner, you will surely have strangers come to the house.

It is very unlucky to burn green elder.

If a goose begins to sit on her eggs when the wind is in the east, she will sit five weeks before she hatches.

Never begin any bit of work on a Friday.

If you swear, you will catch no fish.

If you do not baste the goose on Michaelmas-day, you will want money all the year.

Every person must have some part at least of his dress new on Easter Sunday, or he will have no good fortune that year.

You should always burn a tooth when it is drawn, because, if a dog should find it and eat it, you would have dog's teeth come in its place.

If you eat the marrow of pork you will go mad.

If a servant burns her clothes on her back, it is a sign that she will not leave her place.

* If you make your bed at bedtime, you will look fair in the morning.

In dressing a wound, you must be careful that the old plaster be not burnt; if it is, the wound will not heal. It must always be buried.

---

* It is useless to make it earlier; if you do the fairies will pull it to pieces.
                                                            Mr. Redstone.

Every particle of the leaves or berries of the holly, or other evergreens, with which the house was dressed at Christmas, must be removed on Candlemas Eve. If they are suffered to remain, some misfortune will certainly happen to the family.

If a person is stabbed by a thorn, and can draw it out of the flesh, he must bite the thorn, and then the wound will not fester.

You must never burn the withes (or bands) of the faggots.

Friday is either a very fine or a very wet day.

To put on your stockings inside outwards is a sign of good luck.

Forby, vol. ii, p. 413.

It is considered very unlucky to receive confirmation from the Bishop's *left* hand, those so unfortunate being "doomed on the spot to single blessedness."

J. T. Varden. "E. A. Handbook," p. 108.

The following incidents of ordinary life are accounted "lucky":—
To find a horseshoe, or a piece of metal, if only a pin.

. . . To carry a crooked coin in the pocket. To have a small spider called the "Moneyspinner" descend upon you.

. . . To see two crows *sitting* in the road; very lucky indeed if six are met with in the same place. . . .

"Bad luck" is predicted by the following:—

To come back after once starting on a journey, but the evil may be averted if you sit down in the house for a minute or so; to watch anyone out of sight; to meet a weasel, a hare, or an old woman; to see two sticks lying across in your path; to begin work or go on a journey on Friday; to spill salt, cross knives or spoons; but the bad luck predicted by the first omen may be averted by throwing some of the spilt salt over the *left* shoulder; to help a person to salt;

> " Help me to salt,
> Help me to sorrow."

To walk under a ladder; to see one crow sitting in the road; to pluck the first primrose that blooms in the garden, and carry it into the house; to bring wild flowers into the house.

Sundry other apparently trivial events have also their mystical significance, thus :—

If the foot itches you will soon tread on strange ground; if the right hand itches you will soon take money; but if the left hand itches, you will soon pay money away; if you shiver, some one is walking over your future grave; a flake of soot on the grate indicates the same; if hens are set on an even number of eggs, there will be no chickens; if the first bunch of primroses brought into the house contain less than thirteen, so many eggs only will each hen or goose lay; snakes can only die at night if even they be cut into a dozen pieces.

A Suffolk rhyme teaches us the significance of the "wear of shoes":

> " Tip at the toe, live to see woe;
> Wear at the side, live to be a bride;
> Wear at the ball, live to spend all;
> Wear at the heel, live to save a deal."

J. T. Varden. " E. A. Handbook," p. 115.

Clothes.—It is lucky to put on any article of dress, particularly stockings, inside out; but if you wish the omen to hold good, you must continue to wear the reversed portion of your attire in that condition, till the regular time comes for putting it off, that is, either bed-time or "cleaning yourself." If you set it right you will "change the luck." It will be of no use to put on anything with the wrong side out *on purpose*.

The clothes of the dead will never wear long. When a person dies, and his or her clothes are given away to the poor, it is frequently remarked: "Ah! they may look very well, but they won't wear: they belong to the dead."

If a mother gives away *all* the baby's clothes she has (or the cradle), she will be sure to have another baby, though she may have thought herself above such vanities.

If a girl's petticoats are longer than her frock, that is a sign that her father loves her better than her mother does. . . .

If you would have good luck, you must wear something new on " Whitsun-Sunday " (pronounced Wissun Sunday). . . . A glance

round a church or Sunday-school in Suffolk, on Whitsunday, shows
very plainly that it is the day chosen for beginning to wear new
" things."

> *Suffolk.*   C. W. J.   " Book of Days," vol. ii, p. 322.

A bride on her wedding day should wear :

> " Something new,
> Something blue,
> Something borrowed."

> From Mr. Redstone.

The big blue apron worn by Suffolk cottage women is called by
them a " mantle."   It is considered an omen of ill-luck if their
mantle strings come untied.

> *Ibid.*

If a fire does not burn well, and you want to " draw it up,"
you should set the poker across the hearth, with the fore part
leaning across the top bar of the grate, and you will have a good
fire . . . but you must not . . . refuse to give time to the charm
to work.   For a charm it is, the poker and top bar combined
forming a cross and so defeating the malice . . . of the witches
and demons who preside over smoky chimneys. . . .

> *Suffolk.*   C. W. J.   " Book of Days," vol. ii, p. 105.

The price of corn rises and falls with Barton Mere—an eccentric
piece of water, which varies in size 'from twelve to fourteen acres
to a small pond, and is sometimes entirely dried up.   It lies about
four miles from Bury St. Edmunds, and a worthy old farmer, now
deceased, used frequently to ride to Barton Mere to observe the
state of the water there, before proceeding to Bury Market.

> *Ibid.* p. 322.

If the raindrops hang on the window, more will come to join
them.

> *Ibid.*

Cottagers even now always open doors during a tempest to let the
lightning out.

Beds must never be stuffed with wild birds' feathers, or sleep will be uncomfortable on them.

It never rains fast on the top of the church steeple.

Servants are told not to burn the withies with which faggots are tied, or the bread that is baked will be holey.

You must never burn green leaves or twigs, or ill-luck will attend you.

Take notice how the first foal of the year that you see, stands. If it is with the head towards you, good luck will be yours through the year; if the tail is towards you, bad luck.

From Mr. Manfred Biddell, of Playford.

Divination by Bible and Key. — When any property has been stolen, and a strong suspicion attaches to a particular person, against whom no positive evidence can be obtained, recourse is sometimes had to this mode of divination, which is performed in two different ways. In both of them the key of the church door and the church bible are the instruments employed. In one way of performing the ceremony, the suspected person and the owner of the stolen goods are the only agents. The key is inserted between the leaves of the bible, with the bow and part of the stalk protruding at one end. The book is then tied together very tightly, so that its weight may be supported by the key. The bible is then set on the other end, and is raised from the ground by the supposed thief and the person robbed, each supporting the weight by one or two fingers placed under the bow of the key, opposite to each other. Whilst the book is thus suspended between them, a form of adjuration is pronounced with due solemnity; and it is believed that, if the suspected person be guilty, the bible will of itself turn towards him, and as it were point out the culprit.

The other mode of divination is used when the suspicion is divided amongst many. The parties suspected are arranged round a table, on which is laid the bible with the key upon it. The owner of the stolen goods then takes the key by the middle, and gives it a strong twirl, so that it turns round several times. The person opposite to whom it stops is the thief.

Forby, appendix, vol. ii, p. 399.

Opening the Bible on New Year's Day.—This superstitious practice is still in common use, and much credit is attached to it. It is usually set about with some little solemnity, on the morning of New Year's Day before breakfast, as the ceremony must be performed fasting. The bible is laid on the table unopened; and the parties who wish to consult it are then to open it in succession. They are not at liberty to choose any particular part of the book, but must open it at random, or (as we should say) "*promiscuously.*" Wherever this may happen to be, the inquirer is to place his finger on any chapter contained in the two open pages, but without any previous perusal or examination. The chapter is then read aloud, and commented upon by the company assembled. It is believed that the good or ill fortune, the happiness or misery of the consulting party, during the ensuing year, will in some way or other be described and foreshewn by the contents of the chapter. Of course a good deal of perverse ingenuity is often exercised in twisting and accommodating the sacred texts to the fears or wishes of the consulters; and some have made themselves very wretched, when they have unfortunately opened on any of the prophetic denunciations of divine vengeance. If the chapter happens to contain nothing remarkable, it is concluded that no material change in the circumstances of the enquirer will take place within the year. The reader will probably require little argument to convince him that these modes of divination have descended to us from our Puritanical ancestors.

Ibid. p. 400.

Persons will take the Bible to bed with them on New Year's Eve, and as soon as they awake after twelve o'clock, they open it at random in the dark, mark a verse with their thumb or stick a pin through a verse, turn down a corner of the page, and replace the

14 ⁂

book under the pillow. That verse is supposed to be a prophecy of destiny (good or bad) during the coming year.

"The New Suffolk Garland," p. 179.

Childermas Day.—On whatever day of the week the Anniversary of the Holy Innocents (December 28th) may fall, that same day in every week through the ensuing year, is called Childermas Day. It is "Dies nefastus." Any new undertaking begun upon it will surely fail; and any disaster, which may befal any one, is easily accounted for. That this strange extension of the term "the Mass of Children" beyond its own proper day, existed above an hundred years ago, appears from the paper in the Spectator, No. 7. There was then, as now, a Childermas-day * in every week.

Forby, vol. ii, p. 405.

The Twelve Signs.—We still cling to the notion of planetary influence on the human body. And though the progress of refinement has divested our Almanacks of their formerly indispensable ornament —the figure of a naked man pierced through with darts—yet the doctrine of the "Dominion of the moon on man's body, passing through the twelve zodiacal constellations" (as Francis Moore expresses it) has even now many believers. It is considered a matter of imprudence, if not of danger, to tamper with any part of the body on the day when the column of that sage physician shows it to be under the dominion of the stars; or as our phrase is, "*when the sign lies in it.*" Perhaps our opinion upon this subject may be best explained by an example: About the close of the last century, a medical practitioner of great eminence in Suffolk sent a purge to a patient, and desired him to take it immediately. On the following day he called at his house, and inquired how it had operated. The patient (a substantial farmer) said he had not taken

---

* "Thursday!" says she, "No, child, if it please God, you shall not begin upon Childermas Day; tell your writing-master that Friday will be soon enough." I was reflecting with myself on the oddness of her fancy, and wondering that anybody would establish it as a rule, to lose a day in every week.—C. "The Spectator," Thursday, March 1, 1710–11, No. 7.

it; and upon the doctor's remonstrating against this disobedience, the sick man gravely answered, "That he had looked into his Almanack, and seeing the sign lay in 'Bowels,' he thought *that*, and the physic together, would be too much for him."

Nor are the stars believed to influence the human body only, but to have an equal effect upon brutes. A prudent dairy-wife would never wean a calf when the sign was in the head, lest it should go dizzy; and the author well remembers to have heard a wealthy yeoman inquire of a farrier, when he would perform a certain operation on his colt. The leech assumed a most oracular look, and answered with great gravity, that "he would just step home, and see how the sign lay, and would then let him know."

Ibid. p. 404.

A Suffolk Song.

There was a man lived in the West,
 Limbo clashmo!
There was a man lived in the West,
He married the wuman that he liked best,
With a ricararo, ricararo, milk in the morn
 O' dary mingo.

He married this wuman and browt her hom,
 Limbo clashmo!
He married this wuman and browt her hom,
And set her in his best parlour rom,
With a ricararo, ricararo, milk in the morn
 O' dary mingo.

My man and I went to the fowd,
 Limbo clashmo!
My man and I went to the fowd,
And ketcht the finest wuther that we could howd,
With a ricararo, ricararo, milk in the morn
 O' dary mingo.

We fleed this wuther and browt him hom,
 Limbo, clashmo!
We fleed this wuther and browt him hom,
Ses I, Wife, now yeuar begun yar doon,
With a ricararo, ricararo, milk in the morn
 O' dary mingo.

> I laid this skin on my wife's back,
> 　　Limbo clashmo !
> I laid this skin on my wife's back,
> And on to it I then did swack,
> With a ricararo, ricararo, milk in the morn
> 　　O' dary mingo.
>
> I 'inted har with ashen ile,
> 　　Limbo clashmo !
> I 'inted har with ashen ile,
> Till she could both brew, bake, wash and bile,
> With a ricararo, ricararo, milk in the morn
> 　　　O' dary mingo—mingo.

A Suffolk Man. "Suffolk Notes and Queries,"
Ipswich Journal, 1877.

Local Prophecies.—Some years since a friend showed me the following lines, which he said he copied from an old Court Book of the Manor of Shimpling Thorne, between Bury St. Edmund's and Sudbury :—

> " Twixt Lopham forde and Shimpling Thorne,
> England shall be woonn and lorne.
> 　　　　　　　　　W.

"The East Anglian," or " Notes and Queries."
vol. i, p. 3, 1869.

New Year.—'*First Foot.*'—It is thought lucky, on first going out on New Year's Day, to meet "a big man"; not big in paunch, but in height and breadth, and all the noble proportions "that become a man." Lowestoft is a lucky place to live in for this.

Ed. Fitzgerald. "Sea Words and Phrases." " E.
Anglian," or " Notes and Queries," vol. iv, p. 114.

Cards.—Though often carried on board to pass away the time at All-fours, Don, or Sir-wiser (q.v.), nevertheless regarded with some suspicion when business does not go right. A friend of mine vowed that, if his ill-luck continued, over the cards should go; and over they went.

Opinions differ as to swearing. One captain strictly forbade it on board his lugger; but he also, continuing to get no fish, called out, "Swear away, lads, and see what that'll do."

Ibid. p. 110.

. . . I was assured by an old woman that if a fresh apple was left all night in the room of anyone suffering from small pox, it would be found in the morning to be affected by the disease. It would be, that is, quite corrupt and covered with spots similar to those produced on the body of the patient.

Clare. Oct. 17th. C., "The East Anglian," p. 27.

. . . While walking on our Common, I fell in with a "buoy," who told me to beware of the bull, for he was in a great passion. "Why," said I, "what have you been doing to him?" "Oh!" said he, "I went to him and said:—

> "Tut, prut, bull, you fool,
>   You can't jump over a three-legged stool;"

and that allus do wex 'em so, they don't know what to do for rage!"

Ibid. vol. iii, p. 27.

XV.—NURSERY RHYMES.

A Suffolk Version of a Nursery Rhyme.

I send you a song my little brother learnt from some village lad, but whether it is a true Suffolk song or merely a worthless ballad I cannot say.

> When good King Arthur reigned,
> He was a very good king;
> He kicked three men right out o' the room
> A-cause-a they would na sing.

The first he was a miller;
The second he was a weaver;
The third he was a little tailor;
And they all rose up together;

The miller, he stole corn;
The weaver, he stole yarn;
And the tailor, he stole a roll o' broad cloth
To keep these three rogues warm.

The miller was grinding his corn,
The weaver was spinning his yarn,
And a hen ran away with the little tailor
With the broad cloth under his arm.

> A. W. T. "Suffolk Notes and Queries," Ipswich
> Journal, 1877.

THE CUCKOO.

" In April—'a shake 'as bill,
In May—'a pipe all day,
In June—'a change 'as tune,
In July—awah 'a fly,
Else in August—awah 'a must."

> Moor. "Suffolk Words and Phrases," p. 1.

" The dow she dew no sorrow know,
Until she dew a *benten* go."

That is, until other food failing, she be forced to betake herself
to the seeding *Bentles*,* where she finds but scurvy fare.

> *Ibid.* p. 25.

Barnabee.—The golden-bug or lady-bird: also Bishop-barney: . . .
this pretty little and very useful insect, is tenderly regarded by
our children. One settling on a child is always sent away with
this sad valediction:—

" Gowden-bug, Gowden-bug, fly awah home;
Yar house is bahnt deown an yar children all gone."

—It is sure to fly off on the third repetition.

> *Ibid.* p. 15.

---

* Bentles. Sandy land by the sea, where Bents—*triticum juncium*—grow.

An old labourer at Grundisburgh adds the two following lines
to the above :—

> " Fly to the East, and fly to the West,
> Fly to the home that you like best."

Camilla Gurdon.

NURSERY RHYMES.

(From a Grundisburgh Child.)

> " Hod-ma-Dod, Hod-ma-Dod,
> Stick out your horns,
> Here come an old beggar
> To cut off your corns."

> " Mrs. Mason broke a bason,
> Mrs. Frost asked her how much it cost,
> Mrs. Brown said 'half-a-crown,'
> Mrs. Flory said 'what a story.' "

> " Tiddle Wink, the Barber,
> Went to shave his father,
> The razor slipped and cut his life,
> Tiddle Wink, the Barber."

> " The man in the moon
> Came down too soon,
> To ask his way to Norwich.
> The man in the South
> Burnt his mouth
> With eating cold Plum Porridge."

> " There was an old woman
> Who lived in Dundee,
> And in her back garden
> There grew a plum-tree ;
> The plums they grew rotten
> Before they grew ripe,
> And she sold them three farthings a pint."

> " Dimmitee, Dimmitee Dot,
> The mouse ran up the clock.
> The clock struck one,
> And down she come,
> Dimmitee, Dimmitee Dot."

" I had a little pony.
  His name was Nobby Gray.
  His head was stuffed with pea straw,
  His arms were made of hay.
  He could nimble, he could trot,
  He could carry the mustard pot
  All round the chimney pot.
        I, gee wow."

" Yankee Doodle came to Town,
  And how do you think they serv'd him ?
  One took his bag, and one his scrip,
  The quicker for to starve him."

" I had a little nut tree
  And nothing would it bear,
  But a golden nutmeg
  And a silver pear.
  The King of Spain's daughter
  Came to visit me,
  And all for the sake of my little nut tree."

" There was an Old Man and he went mad
  He jumped into a Biscuit Bag ;
  The Biscuit Bag it was so full
  He jumped onto the Roaring Bull ;
  The Roaring Bull it was so fat
  He jumped into a Gentleman's Hat ;
  The Gentleman's Hat it was so fine
  He jumped into a Glass of Wine ;
  The Glass of Wine it was so clear
  He jumped into a Barrel of Beer ;
  The Barrel of Beer it was so thick
  He jumped on top of the Broom Stick ;
  The Broom Stick it was so rotten,
  That it let him down to the bottom."

OMENS (see Animal, Death, Miscellaneous).

XVI.—PROVERBS AND SIMILES.

"Pretty is what pretty dü."

"Self's allers at home"—heard by me in a sea-board Suffolk parish.

"If that was to rain bread and milk [various reading, 'puddens'] next thing he'd want 'ud be for't to rain a spūne [v.r., 'spünes']."

"He make rats and mice," *i.e.* Practically recognises distinctions between two classes, which the *lower* of them tries to fancy on a level. It was applied to a friend of mine on the border of "the tew counties," who, to avoid the certainty of discomfort and the risk of suffocation at his tithe dinner, tried to meet his large and small farmers on successive days, instead of in one close-packed mass. "But the joskins was staunch, and he found 'twouldn't dü."

"He never give a apple, but what he mean to get a orchard."

"I tell that fellow Dan'ls that job o' his kinder stink o' thyme (time)." This remark was addressed by the most indefatigable of farm-bailiffs—who was always up at four a.m., and expected everyone to move at *his* pace—to a rather dilatory labourer.

"He eat the calf i' the cow's belly," *i.e.* Anticipates his income.

"An Adoptive Sandboy." "Suffolk Notes and Queries," Ipswich Journal.

PROVERBS, ETC.

"If the hen does not prate, she will not lay," *i.e.* Scolding wives make the best housewives.

"If it won't pudding, it will froize," * *i.e.* If it won't do for one thing it will do for another.

"His religion is copyhold, or he has not taken it up." This is said of one who never goes to any place of worship.

"For want of company welcome trumpery."

"A wheelwright's dog is a carpenter's uncle," *i.e.* A bad wheelwright makes a good carpenter.

---

* Froize, s. a pancake.—Forby, vol. i, p. 123.

"You must do as they do at the Hoo; what you can't do in one day, you must do in two."

"He is in his own clothes." This is a term of defiance. Let him do as he pleases; I fear him not.

"A lie made out of the whole stuff," *i.e.* Without any foundation.

"I'll give him a kick for a culp," *i.e.* A Roland for an Oliver.

"Laurence has got hold of him," *i.e.* He is lazy. "Lazy Laurence" was one of the alliterative personifications, which our ancestors were so fond of.

"Hitty-missey, as the blind man shot the crow," *i.e.* accidentally.

"It is a poor dog that does not know 'come out,'" *i.e.* He is foolish who does not know when to desist.

"Everything has an end, and a pudding has two." In explanation of this it must be observed that our Suffolk puddings are not round but long; they are sometimes called leg-puddings, from their resemblance to the human leg . . . in High Suffolk the poke-pudding is still held in high esteem.

"His word is as good as his bond." This is said ironically, when both are worthless.

"Nothing turns sourer than milk," *i.e.* A mild, good-humoured man is most determined, when he is thoroughly provoked.

"There is no fence against a flail," *i.e.* You cannot guard against the attacks of a person who utters blunt unwelcome truths, without any restraint from good manners.

"She looked as if butter would not melt in her mouth, but cheese would not have choked."

"You must eat another yard of pudding first," *i.e.* You must wait till you grow older.

"You must hunt squirrels, and make no noise," *i.e.* If you wish to succeed in an enquiry, you must go quietly about it.

"It is a good thing to eat your brown bread first," *i.e.* If you are unfortunate in the early part of life, you may hope for better success in future.

"Deal with an honest man as you would with a rogue," *i.e.* Do not omit all necessary precautions in business, because a man has the character of being honest.

"The dog that fetches will carry," *i.e.* A tale-bearer will tell tales *of* you, as well as *to* you.

"I was not born in a wood to be scared by an owl," *i.e.* I am not so easily frightened as you may imagine.

"Sorrow rode in my cart." It means to express, I did ill, but I had reason to repent it afterwards.

"His lies are latticed lies, and you may see through them."

"Little knocks rive great blocks;" *i.e.* Steady perseverance with little means, gets through great difficulties.

"His eyes draw straws," *i.e.* He is sleepy. When a person's eyes are nearly closed, he appears to see small rays of light, like straws.

"I will come when the cuckoo has pecked up the dirt," *i.e.* in the Spring.

"Nip a nettle hard and it will not sting you," *i.e.* Strong and decided measures are best with troublesome people.

"'What's her's is mine; what's mine is my own,' quoth the husband."

"You had better be drunk than drowned," *i.e.* It is better to exceed in wine now and then, than to be constantly drinking largely of weak liquors.

"He is a crust of the law; he will never know a crumb of it."

"Your conscience is made of stretching leather."

"There is more of Sampson than of Solomon in him," *i.e.* Great bodily strength but little sense.

"He is a Walberswick whisperer; you may hear him over to Southwold." Walberswick and Southwold are two sea-port towns in Suffolk, situated on opposite sides of the mouth of the river Blyth, and distant nearly a mile from each other. It is of course intended to describe an audible whisperer.

"You may know a carpenter by his chips." This is usually applied to great eaters, who leave many bones on their plate.

"Elbow-grease gives the best polish," *i.e.* Hard rubbing makes furniture look brighter; generally, industry is the surest road to success.

"The miller's boy said so," *i.e.* It was matter of common report.

"She is fond of gape-seed," *i.e.* Of staring at everything that passes.

"To laugh like Robin Good-fellow," *i.e.* A long, loud, hearty, horse-laugh. Thus the memory of the merry goblin still lives amongst us. But though his mirth be remembered, his drudgery is forgotten. He is even forgotten in the nursery.

"He has got his jug," *i.e.* Not so much drink as he could have swallowed, but as much as he can fairly carry. .

"To have the hands of one," *i.e.* To have the advantage of him.

"There are more that know Tom Fool than Tom Fool knows," *i.e.* Persons in public situations are known by many whom they are unacquainted with.

"To go down the red lane," *i.e.* to be swallowed.

"The beard will pay for the shaving." This is used when a person is paid for his labour by taking part, or the whole, of that which he is employed about; as cutting bushes, etc. In general it means, the work will produce enough to pay itself.

"There is a good steward abroad when there is a wind-frost," *i.e.* You have no occasion to look to your labourers, they must work to keep themselves warm.

"There is a deal of difference between go and gow," * *i.e.* between ordering a person to do a thing, and going with him to see him do it, or doing it with him.

"God's lambs will play." An apology for riotous youth; probably it was originally a sneer at some unlucky Puritan, who had been detected in some indiscretion.

"I gave it him as it came from the mill," *i.e.* Undressed; the bran and flour mixed together. It means I spoke my mind plainly, and without dressing it up.

"If the cat's away, the mice will play;" *i.e.* If the master is out of the way, servants will be idle.

"To make one eat *humble* pie," *i.e.* To make him lower his tone and be submissive. It may possibly be derived from the "umbles" of the deer, which were the perquisite of the huntsman . . . . . *umble-pie*, the food of inferiors.

---

* gow, v. let us go; an abbreviation of "go we," the plur. imper. of the verb to go.—Forby, vol. ii, p. 133.

"There's no hoe in them," *i.e.* You cannot stop them; they don't know when to leave off. "They fight without hoe." Lord Berner's Froissart.

"You can't make a silk purse of a sow's ear." . . . .

"It will take the gilding off the gingerbread," *i.e.* It will reduce his profits; he will make little of it.

"To stand holes," *i.e.* To continue as you are; probably borrowed from Cribbage, Fair Play, or some such game.

"Within a hog's gape," *i.e.* Very near; within a little.

"He may well be musical, for he walks upon German flutes." This is often applied to a spindle-shanked musician.

"He has swallowed shame, and drank after it," *i.e.* He has no sense of shame left.

"He does the devil's work for nothing." This is usually said of a common swearer.

"She that's fair, and fair would be, must wash herself with fumitory."

"The man was hanged that left his liquor." This is used as a persuasive to drink, and is said to be derived from the following circumstances. It was the custom to present a cup of wine to criminals on their way to the gallows; one poor fellow who was going to execution refused to stop and drink it. He went on, and was hanged; but just after he was turned off came a reprieve, which would have been in time to save his life, if "he had not left his liquor."

"To lay the stool's foot in water." To make preparation for company. It is derived from the custom of washing brick floors; an operation always performed on the very day company is expected, by many of our "tidy" housewives, with whom wet and clean are synonymous.

"You will catch more flies with a spoonful of honey than with a gallon of vinegar," *i.e.* Kind language prevails more than sharp reproof.

"Little fish are sweet." It means small gifts are always acceptable.

"A lame tongue gets nothing."

1 5

"Go to Bungay, to get new-bottomed." The explanation given of this common saying is, that people broke at Beccles, and when the navigation was opened and improved, removed to Bungay, and throve there. But the saying is probably much older than the navigation. Certainly there are few market towns in which such fortunes have been acquired.

"As bad as marrying the devil's daughter, and living with the old folks." This strange saying is commonly applied to a person who has made unpromising connections in marriage.

"I made my obedience to him, but he would neither speak nor grunt." This is said when a superior passes without returning your civility; and on the same occasion another very common expression is, "A hog would have grunted."

"A ground sweat cures all disorders," *i.e.* In the grave all complaints cease from troubling.

"Give him that which costs you nothing," *i.e.* civility.

"He does not know great A from the gable end of a house."

"He laughs on the wrong side of his face," *i.e.* He affects a laugh when he is disposed to cry.

"It is better to wear up with work than with rust."

"He was meant for a gentleman, but was spoilt in the making."

"He lies bare of a suit," *i.e.* He has no money.

"He will make a tight old man." This is said of a lazy fellow who does not hurt himself with work.

"He has laid a stone at my door," *i.e.* by way of memorandum not to knock at it again; in the modern cant phrase, "He has cut me."

"He has made a hole in his manners." This expression is much like Cotgrave's "casse maurs."

Forby, vol. ii, p. 427.

"If it warn't for hope the heart 'ud die."

(From the old Gardener at Grundisburgh Hall.)

"God never pays his debts with money." Said of any bad person who falls ill, or meets with misfortunes.

(From the Rev. S. Hooke, Rector of Clopton.)

" 'A spend everything 'a can rap and rend." That is, all he can get. It is probably *rip* and *rend*—both words meaning tear and waste.

Ed. Moor. " Suffolk Words and Phrases," p. 308.

"Happy is the bride that the sun shines on ; happy is the corpse that the rain rains on."

Ibid. p. 163.

"When ye lah an egg, tho' ta be a' gowd, don't *cackle*."

Ibid. p. 62.

" As dry as a Hambuck." " His legs are like Hambucks." Hambuck : the dry fibrous stalk of hemp, after having been peeled.

Ibid. p. 190.

A Suffolk Proverb.

" Singers and ringers are little home bringers."

A. W. T., " Suffolk Notes and Queries," Ipswich Journal.

" Thin as a rake " is not an unfrequent comparison with us : which I should, unaided, have thought meant simply as the shin handle, or *stale*, as we call it, of the rake. On this passage in Coriolanus i, 1—

> " Let us revenge this with our pikes ere we become *rakes*,"

commentators have, and I cannot but deem needlessly, put forth a deal of learning. Steevens has I think hit on the author's meaning, which in Suffolk we should say is " as plain as a pike-staff," and shows the proverb " thin as a rake " to be as old as Shakespeare's day, and that he referred merely to the paper-handled tool. . . . I may note that the long handled tool that we call a *pitch-fork* . . . used it appears to be called a *pike*, and is still called so in Devonshire.

Ed. Moor, p. 305.

" His tongue moves like a beggar's *clap-dish*."
Clap-dish, s. . . . It was a dish, or rather box, with a movabe

lid, carried by the beggars at that time, to attract notice by the
noise it made, and to bring people to their doors. . . .

Forby, vol. i, p. 65.

" Her eyes are as black as *sloons* "—sloes.

Ed. Moor, p. 363.

" Pale as a *deusan*."
Deusan, s. a hard sort of apple which keeps a long time, but
turns pale and shrivels. . . . Fr. *deux ans.*

Forby, vol. i, p. 92.

" As yulla as a peagle " is said of a sallow atrabilious person.
Peagle : the cowslip.

Ed. Moor, p. 268.

Conger-eel.—Sometimes cast ashore, alive and kicking, in winter.
I was wondering how so strong a fish suffered himself to be so
stranded, and was told (at Felixstowe) that it was because of the
Conger " blinding himself by striking at the stars."

Ed. FitzGerald. *Works,* vol. ii, p. 466.

" Deep as the North-Star ; " said (by the conger-eel man) of
a very *wide-awake* babe four months old.

Ibid.

" The night's as dark as black hogs."

Ibid.

" Flat as a dab," the sea calm-flat, as the flat fish, so commonly
called.

Ibid.

Willock.—A Guillemot, I am told. The same bird that, " after
shutting the door after him," presents the kitty with the fish he
has re-appeared with. This is not the action of an ill-mannered
bird ; nor have I seen anything wild in his demeanour. Yet,
they say, " Mad as a willock."

Ibid.

Dutch Uncle.—"There were the squires on the bench, but I took heart, and talked to 'em like a Dutch Uncle." This, I trust, opens a wide field for conjecture.

Ibid.

Neighbour's Fare.—Doing as well as one's neighbours. "I mayn't make a fortune, but I look for neighbour's fare nevertheless."

Ibid.

Shim-Shimmer.—The glitter of fish coming above water, into the net. When the mackerel men—after many and many an empty net—come to draw in one with a shimmer of fish in it, they say—

> "There's a white,
> And a shim,
> And another after him;
> And a white,
> And a lily-white,
> And a scrunck-ho!"

Ibid.

"You're giving extra good measure, Mrs. Spalding."
"A-well, my pore father he used to say, 'Hape it up Maw'r, hape it up:

> "Good weight an' measure
> Is hivenly treasure."

A. W. T. "Suffolk Notes and Queries," Ipswich Journal, 1877.

"As thick as todge."

A Suffolk man. *Ibid.*

"As blue as Wad." Wad s. Woad.

Forby, vol. ii, p. 366.

"As white as Nip." Nep. Nip. s. the herb cat-mint, nepeta cataria, Lin.

Ibid. p. 230.

"As thick as Loblolly."

"East Anglian in Suffolk Notes and Queries," Ipswich Journal.

Loblolly, s. neither water gruel nor any particular seafaring dish as Todd's Johnson makes it. With us, as in Exmore, it means, "any odd mixture of spoon-meat," provided only that it be very thick.

Forby, vol. ii, p. 198.

In years long ago, I remember the old quatrain which we as children used to repeat, when a piece of paper was burnt, and we noted how the sparks on the burnt and blackened paper kept moving about, and at last went out one by one. The lines were as follows :—

> " There goes the parson,
> And there goes the clerk;
> And there go the people
> Out in the dark."

Senex. "Suffolk Notes and Queries," Ipswich Journal.

At the rectory gatherings on Christmas night, Will was one of the principal singers; his *chefs-d'œuvre* "Oh! silver (query *Sylvia*) is a charming thing" and "The Helmingham Wolunteers." That famous corps was raised by Lord Dysart, to repel "Bony's" threatened invasion; its drummer was John Noble, afterwards the wheelwright in Monk Soham. Once after drill, Lord Dysart said to him: "You played that very well, John Noble;" and "I know't, my lord, I know't," was John's answer—an answer that has passed into a Suffolk proverb, "I know't, my lord, I know't, as said John Noble."

Francis Hindes Groome. "A Suffolk Parson." Blackwood's Edinburgh Magazine, March, 1891, p. 318.

A Yarmouth *Capon.*—That is, a red herring: more herrings being taken than capons bred here.

Ray. "A Complete Collection of English Proverbs," p. 225.

A London *Cockney.*—This nickname is more than four hundred years old. For when Hugh Bigot added artificial fortifications to his naturally strong castle of Bungey in Suffolk, he gave out this rhyme, therein vaulting it for impregnable.

" Were I in my Castle of Bungey
Upon the river of Waveney,
I would ne care for the King of Cockney,

meaning thereby King Henry II., then quietly possessed of London, whilst some other places did resist him : though, afterwards, he so humbled this Hugh, that he was fain with large sums of money, and pledges for his loyalty, to redeem this his Castle from being razed to the ground. I meet with a double sense of this word Cockney.—1. One *coax'd* and *cocquer'd*, made a wanton or nestle-cock, delicately bred and brought up, so as when grown up to be able to endure no hardship. 2. One utterly ignorant of country affairs, of husbandry and houswivery as there practised. The original thereof, and the tale of the citizen's son, who knew not the language of a Cock, but called it *neighing*, is commonly known.

Ibid. p. 252.

" Before the Normans into England came, Bentley was my seat, and Tollemache was my name."

> Higson's MSS. Coll. No. 72. Bentley in Suffolk, near Ipswich. " English Proverbs " and " Proverbial Phrases," arranged and annotated by W. Carew Hazlitt. J. Russell Smith, London, 1869.

Ash Week, the first week in Lent.
Old Mothers' Rock-stones, old wives' fables.

> (Paulinus. " Suffolk Notes and Queries," Ipswich Journal.)

"My ancient authority" (*i.e.* "one who dated from the early part of the last century ") " would frequently say, if a person was relating a fabulous tale, 'There, that's only the old woman's Rock Staff,*

---

* Rock-Rock-Staff, s. a distaff; from which, as we are told in Todd's Johnson, the wool *was* spun " by twirling a ball below." It *is* spun, to this day, by being drawn out and formed into yarn by the finger and thumb, and pressed by the hand on the trip-skin, against which the spindle twirls, by degrees collecting on itself the ball. . . . " An old woman's rock-staff " is a contemptuous expression for a silly superstitious fancy.—Forby, vol. ii, p. 279.

which the old man took for a walking stick, and carried it all over the world.' "

　　　　　'East Anglian.'　"Suffolk Notes and Queries,"
Ipswich Journal.

A White Mary.—" N. M. told me that one day last Spring, when she was walking up the Church Meadow, she had fallen down in a kind of fit; that the night before, when she was just falling off to sleep, she was frightened by some one seeming to stand by her bedside; she did not know whether it was a *White Mary* or not. She put out her hand to push it away. I said, 'I suppose it was what we call nightmare.'"

　　　　　Camfordiensis.　"Suffolk Notes and Queries," Ipswich
Journal.

Cavey—Peccavi.—" A began to cry *Cavey*."—he began to knock under—to moderate.

　　　　　Ed. Moor.　"Suffolk Words and Phrases," p. 72.

Jack at a Pinch.—A sudden unexpected call to do anything. " Well, if I be'ent set tew regular I on't come Jack at a pinch." " Children and chicken are always a-picking."

　　　　　(From Mr. Redstone, Woodbridge.)

Three blue beans in a blue bladder.—What is the origin of this whimsical combination of words, it may not be easy to discover; but at least it is of long standing.

　　F. Hark! doest rattle?
　　S. Yes, like three blue beans in a blue bladder, rattle bladder, rattle.
　　　　　　　　　Old Fortunatus, Anc. Dr. iii, p. 128.

Prior has it in his Alma:

　　　　　" They say—
　　　That putting all his words together,
　　　'Tis three blue beans in one blue bladder."
　　　　　　　　　Cant. i, v. 25.

Thus far Nares. To this I have to add that " three blue beans in one blue bladder, rattle bladder, rattle "—thrice repeated, is an old and frolicksome sort of Suffolk shibboleth, as I can recollect; and is still frequently heard.

Moor, p. 22.

Proud as a Horse.—The Sailor generally regarding that creature as showing so much of the Devil, with all its rearings and prancings, and "Ha, Ha's!" . . .

Ed. FitzGerald. "Sea Words," etc. "E. Anglian" or "Notes and Queries," vol. iv, p. 114.

"Great Ships ask deep Waters."

Ibid. p. 263.

Mitten.—"Dead as a Mitten"—that is the sea phrase. Another article as well appreciated by the Seaman is commonly used for the same comparison ashore. A Game-keeper near Lowestoft was describing how some Dignitary of the Church—he knew not what —was shooting with his Master. Some game—I know not what —was sprung; and the Gamekeeper, at a loss for any correct definition of his man, called out "Blaze away, your Holiness!"— "And blowed if he didn't knock it over as dead as a Biscuit."

Ibid. p. 263.

"A thatch'd church and ivied steeple, a bad parson and wicked people."

W. H. S. "The E. Anglian," vol. iv, p. 168.

XVII.—SLEEP CHARMS.

A popular prayer that is taught to children by some parents is clearly a relic of Roman Catholic times, and has been handed down from a period anterior to the Reformation, for it is an appeal to particular Saints for their intercession with Almighty God. The words are these—

> " Matthew, Mark, Luke and John,
> Bless the bed I lie upon ;
> Four corners to my bed,
> Four angels at its head,
> One to watch, two to pray,
> And one to bear my soul away ;
> God within and God without,
> Sweet Jesus Christ all round about ;
> If I die before I wake
> I pray to God my soul to take."

There is sometimes this ludicrous (?) variation of the fourth line—

> " Four angels all aspread."

"The New Suffolk Garland," p. 178.

The Spell of St. Edmund's Bury.—Wynkyn de Worde put forth the first edition of the Horæ, in this country, relating to the Cathedral Service at Salisbury, under the following title : "Hore beate Marie Virginis ad usum insignio ecclesie Sarum. Londinii per Winandum de Worde. 1502." 4to membran. A copy of this impression, now in the Gough Library at Oxford, and described in Vol. ii, p. 107, of Dibdin's Typographical Antiquities, and in Vol. i, pp. 11, 12, of the 2nd day of his Decameron, contained upon the margin thereof certain written rhymes, in an ancient hand, of a strange mysterious nature : to wit, " the Little Credo," " the White Paternoster," and the following curious spell :—

Peter's Brother where lyest all night ?

Ther as Chryst y God.

What hast in thy honde ? heaven Keyes.

What hast in thy tother ?

Broade booke leaves.

Open heauen gates,

Shutt hell Geates.

Euerie child creepe christ ouer

White Benedictus be in this howse

Euerye night.

Within and without. This howse rounde about,
St. Peter att the one doore,
St. Paule att the other,
St. Michael in the middle
Fyer in the flatt
Chancell-op sbatt
Euerie naugers bore
An Angell before.
　　　　—Amen.

　　　　　　　　　" The Suffolk Garland," p. 354.

A Spell against thieves, to be said three times while walking round the premises :—

In the name of the Father, Son, and Holy Ghost,
This house I bequeath round about,
And all my goods within and without,
In this yard or enclosed piece of land,
Unto Jesus Christ, that died on a tree,
The Father, Son, and Holy Ghost, all Three,
　　　Thieves! Thieves! Thieves!
By virtue of the Blessed Trinity.
That you stir not one foot from this place until the rising of the sun next morning with beams full clear. And this I charge you in the name of the Trinity; Jesus save me and mine from them and fetching. Amen.

　　　　　　Quoted from a note on " Spells " (by G.R.P. in the
　　　　　　Eastern Counties Collectanea), by J. T. Varley,
　　　　　　E. A. Handbook, 1885, p. 100.

A Spell as a protection from Assault. . . .

　　　" Whoever thou art that meanest me ill,
　　　　　Stand thou still !
　　　As the river Jordan did
　　　When our Lord and Saviour, Jesus,
　　　Was baptised therein.
　　　In the name of Father, Son, and Holy Ghost."
　　　　　　　　　　　　　　Amen.

　　　　　　　　　　　　　　　　Ibid.

It is not easy to get hold of spells . . . many people disown any knowledge of Spells, believing there is something "uncanny" in their use.

Ibid.

XVIII.—WEATHER MYTHS.

I still occasionally hear people assert that if a pig is killed while the moon is waning the fat will in cooking shrink.   Their rule therefore is to kill their pigs while the moon is waxing. . . . Reversely, it was believed that there were things which ought to be done while the moon was waning; for instance, you should cut your corns at this time.   The moon is waning.   Growth will then be weak.   They will not wax again rapidly.   The moon that wanes in heaven before our eyes is the cause of all sublunary waning.   Its period of waning is the period of waning in all things.   Therefore, take off your lambs and little pigs while the moon is in this phase.   The secretion of milk in the ewes and the sows will then be more readily staunched.   It is waning time.   It is a bad time for putting up poultry to fatten.   It would be contrary to nature for them to wax at that time.

Some materials for the Hist. of Wherstead, by F. B. Zincke, p. 175.   See Forby. vol. ii, p. 404.

" Sow pease (good trull)
  The moon past full.
  Fine seeds then sow,
  Whilst moon doth grow.
      Tusser. " Five Hundred Points," p. 101.

" Sow peason and beans in the wane of the moon,
  Who soweth them sooner, he soweth too soon,
  That they with the planet may rest and arise,
  And flourish, with bearing most plentifullwise."

Ibid. p. 107.

" Cut all things or gather, the moon in the wane,
  But sow in encreasing, or give it his bane."

Ibid. p. 131.

" In March is good graffing, the skilful do know,
So long as the wind in the east do not blow:
From moon being changed, till past be the prime,
For graffing and cropping, is very good time."

Ibid. p. 127.

The new moon "lying on its back," with the horns of her crescent pointing upwards, is believed to indicate a dry moon[*]; and, on the contrary, when the new moon appears with the horns of the crescent pointing downwards, or as it is locally expressed, "when it hangs dripping," it will be a wet moon.

When the new moon happens on a Saturday, it is superstitiously believed to be a sign of unfavourable weather, thus :

" A Saturday moon—
If it comes once in seven years comes too soon."

And if in addition the full moon falls on a Sunday, it is said :

" Saturday new, Sunday full,
Never was good, and never *wool.*"

There is also a saying that " the sun is always seen on a *Saturday,*" and this is firmly believed by many of the country people. . . . . .
" The New Suffolk Garland," p. 166.

Many persons will courtesy to the new moon on its first appearance, and turn the money in their pockets ' for luck.' Last winter I had a set of rough country lads in a night-school; they happened to catch sight of the new moon through the window, and all (I think) that had any money in their pockets turned it ' for luck.' . . . The boys could not agree what was the right form of words to use on the occasion, but it seemed to be understood that there was a proper formula for it.

Suffolk. C. W. J., "Book of Days," vol. ii, p. 203.

[*] In this position it is supposed to retain the water, which is imagined to be in it, and which would run out if the horns were turned down.—*Suffolk.* C. W. J., "Book of Days," vol. ii, p. 203.

Another superstition was acknowledged by them [*i.e.* a set of rough country lads in a night-school] at the same time—namely, that it was unlucky to see the new moon for the first time through glass. . . .

· · · To see 'the old moon in the arms of the new one' is reckoned a sign of fine weather.

Ibid.

It is lucky to see the moon over your left shoulder.

Forby. "Vocab. of E. Anglia," vol. ii. Appendix.

Weather.

"Evening red, and morning grey
  Send the traveller on his way;
But evening grey, and morning red,
  Send the traveller wet to bed."

"A rainbow at morning
  Is the shepherd's warning;
But a rainbow at night
  Is the shepherd's delight."

A *burr*, that is, a *halo*, round the moon is a sign of rain; if it is large, the proverb is :—

"Far burr, near rain;
  Near burr, far rain."

When a robin sings at the bottom of a bush it betokens bad weather, but if he sings at the top of a bush it will be fair. . . .

"March dry, good rye;
  April wet, good wheat."

When you see the grey "Shepherd's flock" before 8 o'clock in the morning, it will rain before night.

"If it rains before seven
  'Twill cease before eleven."

The sun rising clear in the morning and going to bed again (as it is called) immediately, is a sure indication of a foul day. When

the small clouds are seen scudding before larger ones, they are called
"*water carts*," and rain is sure to follow.

> " When the wind's in the South,
> 'Tis in the rain's mouth ;
> When the wind's in the East,
> 'Tis neither good for man nor beast."

There is also a saying with reference to the new moon, that—

> " When early seen
> 'Tis seldom seen."

" When a cat wipes her face over her ears, it is a sign of fine
weather, and when a cat sits with her back towards the fire, it
is a sign of frost."

> " A fine Saturday, a fine Sunday :
> A fine Sunday, a fine week."

> " If the rainbow comes a night,
> The rain is gone, quite."

> " When it rains with the wind in the East,
> It rains for twenty-four hours at least."

> " May never goes out without a wheat ear."

> " The grass that grows in Janiveer
> Grows no more all the year."

> " Cut your thistles before St. John,
> You will have two instead of one."

> " First comes David, then comes Chad,
> Then comes Winnold as if he were mad."

This alludes to the stormy weather which is common at the
beginning of March.

> "The New Suffolk Garland," collected by John Glyde,
> junior. Printed for the Author, St. Matthew's
> Street, Ipswich, 1866. pp. 166, 167, 168.

> " Rain before seven,
> Fine before eleven."

. . . The character of St. Swithin's Day is much regarded here as a prognostication of fine or wet weather.

. . . The streaks of light often seen when the sun shines through broken clouds are believed to be pipes reaching into the sea, and the water is supposed to be drawn up through them into the clouds, ready to be discharged in the shape of rain.

Suffolk.   C. W. J.   "Book of Days," vol. ii, p. 203.

There is a saying at Woodbridge that where Bromeswell wind is on Ash Wednesday, there it continues to blow for 40 days. It is also called Old Parker's wind. Old Parker, the people say, was a very disagreeable old man, who lived at Bromeswell. His wind is the East Wind.

From Mr. Redstone.

Water-dogs, s. pl. small clouds of irregular but roundish form, and of a darker colour, floating below the dense mass of cloudiness in rainy seasons, supposed to indicate the near approach of more rain.

Forby.   "Vocabulary of East Anglia," vol. ii, p. 369.

Noah's Ark, s. a cloud, appearing when the sky is for the most part clear: much resembling, or at least supposed to resemble, a large boat turned bottom upwards. It is considered as a sure prognostic of rain.

Ibid. p. 233.

It is believed among us that such a cloud immediately preceded and prefigured the deluge, and we still confidently expect rain on its re-appearance.

Ed. Moor.   "Suffolk Words and Phrases," p. 250.

Roger's-Blast, s. a sudden and local motion of the air, not otherwise perceptible but by its whirling up the dust on a dry road in perfectly calm weather, somewhat in the manner of a water-spout. It is reckoned a sign of approaching rain.

Forby, vol. ii. p. 280.

" On Candlemas Day if the sun shines clear,
The shepherd had rather see his wife on her bier."

So many fogs in March, so many frosts in May.

" If the robin sings in the bush,
Then the weather will be coarse ;
But if the robin sings on the barn.
Then the weather will be warm."

A mackerel sky forebodes rain.

When frogs in the grass appear of a bright yellowish green, the weather will be fine; if they are of a dark dirty brown there will be rain.

A wet Sunday, a wet week.

" Sow in the slop,
Heavy at top,"

i.e., wheat sown when the ground is wet, is most productive. Wheat always lies best in wet sheets.

" When the pigeons go a benting,
Then the farmers lie lamenting."

At Old Christmas the days are longer by a cock's stride. A green Christmas, a fat churchyard.

" On Saint Valentine
All the birds of the air in couples do join."

" Saint Matthew
Get candlesticks new.
Saint Matthi
Lay candlesticks by."

" Saint Andrew the King,
Three weeks and three days before Christmas comes in."

On Holy-Rood day the Devil goes a-nutting."

Ibid. p. 415.

Bleuse.—This is a noun formed from ' blue.' It means a bluish mist, not unusual in summer when the temperature suddenly becomes chilled, the sky remaining cloudless. It is supposed to bring a blight. I will give the meaning of the word as it was many years ago explained to me by a Suffolk labourer. I had said to him . . . . "This chilly haze will bring blight." To this he sharply replied, correcting me, "It is no haze." "Well," I enquired, "What is it? It is what people call haze or mist." "No," was his rejoinder, "it is not haze or mist, it is 'blewse.'" "And what," I continued, "is 'blewse'?" "Why," he replied, "everybody knows what 'blewse' is. It is the smoke of the burning mountain."

> "Some materials for the Hist. of Wherstead," by F. B. Zincke, p. 195.

The London Road.—Once on a clear starlight night I said something to a labourer, who happened to be with me, about the Milky Way. "We," he interposed, "don't call it by that name. We call it the London Road." I supposed at the moment that this merely meant that from the neighbourhood where we were it was parallel to the direction of the London Road. It was for this reason that Watling Street (the Roman Road from London to Wroxeter) and the Milky Way were once interchangeable appellations. On continuing the conversation, however, I found that this was the smallest part of the reason why the luminous celestial belt had received this strange local appellation. The date of our conversation was in the days before railways, when the upper ten thousand posted to and fro, and there was a great deal of traffic by night in carriages and wagons. "Its name," he explained, "is the London Road, because it is the light of the lamps of the carriages and wagons that are travelling to and from London."

> *Ibid.* p. 197.

Milkmaids' Path.—The milky way; as if the heavenly milkmaid had spilt her pail as she crossed over. Not so uncouth a fancy!

> "Sea Words and Phrases along the Suffolk coast," p. 7.

XIX.—WELL WORSHIP.

Of the Holy Wells near Ipswich there remains only the name, which still distinguishes some clear springs. There is also, on Mr. Milner-Gibson Cullum's property near Bury a spot named Holy Well, but no traditions concerning either place survive.

Camilla Gurdon.

. . . In a low part of the lane that leads from *the Green* towards Whepstead, is a spring that rises to a level with the road : it had formerly a margin of free-stone, part of which still remains, inscribed :

> " Jacob's well—
> Empty the sea,
> And empty me."

Its boast is not a vain one ; for it was never exhausted during the late succession of remarkably dry summers.

Sir J. Cullum's " Hist. and Antiq. of Hawstead," p. 6.

XX.—WITCHCRAFT.

As early as the reign of Henry the Sixth, " Margery Jourdemayn, the famous witch of Eye," was employed by the Duchess* of

> " A sort of naughty persons, lewdly bent,—
> Under the countenance and confederacy
> Of Lady Eleanor, the protector's wife,
> The ringleader and head of all this rout—
> Have practised dangerously against your State,
> Dealing with witches, and with conjurers ;
> Whom we have apprehended in the fact ;
> Raising up wicked spirits from under ground,
> Demanding of King Henry's life a death,
> And other of your highness' privy council,
> As more at large your grace shall understand."
>
> —Shakespeare. " King Henry VI." Part ii. Act. ii. Sc. 1.

Gloucester, wife of the good Duke Humphrey. . . In the latter part of the last century, however, the immediate neighbourhood of Eye was again distinguished by the residence of a Sybil, who, under the name of "Old Nan Barret," enjoyed for more than forty years a reputation only inferior to that of her renowned predecessor. She was not indeed sought after by royalty, nor probably much known out of "the two counties"; but in them she was held in high veneration, and it was no unusual thing for people to go thirty or forty miles to consult her. . .

The belief that witches are inclined to injure others gratuitously, and of mere malice, appears to be much upon the decline. It was at its greatest height amongst us towards the middle of the seventeenth century. In 1693 a book was published by "Samuel Petts, Minister of the Gospel at Sudbury, in Suffolk," containing a "faithful narrative of the wonderful and extraordinary fits, which Mr. Thomas Spatchett (late of Dunwich and Cookly) was under by witchcraft." It is a thin quarto of thirty-five pages, and proves, curiously enough, the perverse inclination, then prevailing, of imputing any unusual symptoms of disease to witchcraft. In this case also it appears that a confession of her guilt was extorted from the suspected witch. But it should appear that the appetite for judicial murder on this account was glutted, or that courts of justice were not so ready to entertain cases of this kind; for the author feelingly complains, "that notwithstanding what could be witnessed against her, yet she was sent home; and nothing in point of law was done against her." . . .

Sometimes, however, the revenge of witches was exercised rather in a sportive than a malignant spirit : of this an instance was told, and religiously believed, in Norfolk, towards the end of the last century. A farmer's wife had lost some feathers, and consulted the celebrated "Nan Barrett" on the surest mode of recovering them. The Sybil assured her that they should be brought back ; but the niggardly housewife, having obtained this assurance, refused to pay the old woman her accustomed fee. Provoked, as she well might be, at being thus bilked, the prophetess repeated the assurance that the feathers should come back, but added, "that the owner should not be the better for them." The enquirer, however, fully satisfied that she should recover her goods, laughed at the threat, and returned in high glee. . . . As soon as she got home, she called her maids to go to milking; and when they had about half done, hearing a slight noise, she raised her head, and saw her feathers come flying into the milking-yard like a swarm of bees; and, to her great annoyance, beheld them direct their flight towards the milk-pails : thus spoiling at once both milk and feathers. It will readily be imagined that, after this catastrophe, no one ever ventured to defraud Mrs. Barrett of her dues. . . . .

The belief is, that a witch cannot pass over the threshold on which a horseshoe is nailed, with the open part upwards; or at least, that she cannot perform her diabolical feats within the door to which it belongs. . . . . There is, indeed, another prophylactick, but which, from its nature, can only be resorted to in extreme cases. Where a witch is known to harbour resentment against any-one, or to have expressed an intention of doing him an injury, it is held to be a sure preservative, if the party threatened can draw blood from the sorceress : and many a poor old woman has been scarified, from the received opinion that a witch will not " *come to the scratch.*" Next to prevention comes the remedy; and the following is considered as a specific. If in the near neighbourhood, or anywhere indeed within the malignant influence of a known witch, a child is afflicted with an obstinate ague, a great many worms, or any pining sickness; if a calf be dizzy, or a cow " tail-shotten," or have " gargot," or " red-water,"; so that it may *reasonably* be concluded to be bewitched; the most effectual remedy, or mode of exorcism, is to take a quantity of the patient's urine, and boil it with nine nails from as many old horse-shoes. The process is to begin exactly at midnight. The conductress of it is to have an assistant to obey orders, but is to touch nothing herself. . . . . These orders must be conveyed by signs. A single word mars the whole charm. At a certain critical point in the process, when three, five, or seven of the nails have been put in motion at once by the force of the boiling fluid (for some cases are more difficult than others) the spirit is cast out: at which happy moment, the child squalls,

the cow "blores," or the calf "blares"; convalescence immediately
commences of course. The good woman, from whom the author
obtained this valuable information about forty years ago (not immediately, indeed, nor without some little breach of confidence), confirmed
it by recounting a failure that once befell herself. She had prevailed
on a boy to sit up with her. All was going on most prosperously.
The hob-nails were in merry motion. The child in the cradle
squalled. The boy, in a cold sweat, ventured to look behind him;
he was so overpowered with terror, that he forgot all the cautions
he had received, and called to his mistress to look at the little black
thing, which was endeavouring to escape through the keyhole. This
was, no doubt, the evil spirit; which, thus recalled, must have
entered the poor child again, for it certainly never recovered.

At present, indeed, the power principally attributed to witches
amongst us is that of foretelling future events, and of discovering
the possessors of stolen goods.

. . . One circumstance more remains to be mentioned with respect
to witches. It is generally believed that a witch, or wizard, be
his size or corpulence what it may, cannot weigh down the Church
Bible: and many instances might be cited of persons accused of
witchcraft applying to the clergyman of the parish to be allowed
to prove their innocency by this ordeal. This trial, however, is
not considered quite satisfactory when the suspicion is very strong
against the party accused. The only sure criterion by which his
guilt or innocence can be satisfactorily ascertained is still believed
to be by swimming.

Forby. "Vocabulary of East Anglia," Appendix,
vol. ii, pp. 388–398. 1830.

. . . Edmund Beaufort, Duke of Somerset . . . is said to have
consulted Margery Jourdemayne, the celebrated witch of Eye, with
respect to his conduct and fate during the impending conflicts.
She told him that he would be defeated and slain at a castle;
but as long as he arranged his forces and fought in the open
field, he would be victorious and safe from harm. . . . After the
first battle of St. Albans, when the trembling monks crept from

their cells to succour the wounded and inter the slain, they found the dead body of Somerset lying at the threshold of a mean alehouse, the sign of which was a castle. And thus:

> " Underneath an alehouse' paltry sign,
> The Castle in Saint Alban's, Somerset
> Hath made the wizard famous in his death."
>
> —Shakespeare. " King Henry VI." Part ii. Act v. Sc. 3.

" The Book of Days," ed. by R. Chambers, vol. i, p. 399.

SCENE IV.—THE SAME—THE DUKE OF GLOSTER'S GARDEN.

[Enter Margery Jourdain, Hume, Southwell, and Bolingbroke.]

Hume. Come, my masters ; the duchess, I tell you, expects performance of your promises.

Boling. Master Hume, we are therefore provided : Will her ladyship behold and hear our exorcisms ?

Hume. Ay ! what else ? fear you not her courage.

Boling. I have heard her reported to be a woman of an invincible spirit : But it shall be convenient, Master Hume, that you be by her aloft while we be busy below ; and so, I pray you, go in God's name, and leave us. *[Exit Hume.]* Mother Jourdain. be you prostrate, and grovel on the earth : John Southwell, read you ; and let us to our work.

[Enter Duchess, above.]

Duch. Well said, my masters ; and welcome all. To this geer ; the sooner the better.

Boling. Patience, good lady ; wizards know their times :
Deep night, dark night, the silence of the night,
The time of night when Troy was set on fire ;
The time when screech-owls cry, and ban-dogs howl,
And spirits walk, and ghosts break up their graves,
That time best fits the work we have in hand.
Madam, sit you, and fear not ; whom we raise,
We will make fast within a hallow'd verge.

[Here they perform the ceremonies appertaining. and make the circle ; Bolingbroke *or* Southwell *reads* Conjuro te, etc. *It thunders and lightens terribly ; then the Spirit riseth.]*

Spir. Adsum.

M. Jourd. Asmath.
By the eternal God, whose name and power
Thou tremblest at, answer that I shall ask ;
For till thou speak thou shall not pass from hence.

Spir. Ask what thou wilt : That I had said and done !

Boling. " First of the king. What shall of him become ?"

[*Reading out of a paper.*]

Spir. The duke yet lives that Henry shall depose;
But him outlive and die a violent death.

[*As the* Spirit *speaks,* Southwell *writes the answer.*]

Boling. "What fates await the Duke of Suffolk?"
Spir. By water shall he die, and take his end.
Boling. "What shall befall the Duke of Somerset?"
Spir. Let him shun castles;
Safer shall he be upon the sandy plains,
Than where castles mounted stand.
Have done, for more I hardly can endure.
Boling. Descend to darkness, and the burning lake,
False fiend, avoid!

[*Thunder and lightning.* Spirit *descends.*]

—Shakespeare. "King Henry VI.," Part ii. Act 1.

WITCHCRAFT TRIALS.

In 1663, Lowestoft shared the disgrace with Yarmouth and Bury of the infamous witch prosecutions. Hopkins, the witch-finder, went his circuit, causing the death of sixteen unhappy creatures at Yarmouth, forty at Bury, and a number in other towns. At Lowestoft, a Mr. Samuel Pacey, an eminent dissenter, commenced a prosecution against two poor widows for bewitching two of his daughters. They were tried at Bury, before Sir Matthew Hale, condemned and executed.

John Cream Nall. "Chapters on the East Anglian Coast," Part i, pp. 190, 191.

In reference to Hopkins, the Assembly Book of Great Yarmouth records under date Aug. 15th, 1645, as follows:—"Agreed that the gentleman, Mr. Hopkins, employed for discovering and finding out witches, be sent for to town to search for such wicked persons, if any be, and have his fee and allowance for his pains, as he hath in other places."

Ibid. p. 32.

Hopkins was too busy to bestow much time on it, and a staff of four female assistants as searchers and watchers were engaged at a salary of 12d. a day amongst them. The result of their labours was a presentment at the sessions on the 10th of September of that year, of six widows and spinsters for practising witchcraft and sorcery. They were all adjudged to be suspended by the neck, &c., until, &c., which sentence was carried out, one only being respited.

Ibid. p. 93. (Note.)

We arrive now at a melancholy phase in the history of punishments recorded as inflicted in this Borough. I refer to the hanging of witches in the year 1645. It will be interesting to read an extract or two from a book relating to the notorious Matthew Hopkins, commonly called the Witch-finder General. This man was born at Manningtree, in Essex, and was, with some others, commissioned by Parliament in 1644 and two following years, to perform a circuit for the discovery of witches. By virtue of this commission, they went from place to place through many parts of Essex, Suffolk, Norfolk, and Huntingdonshire, and caused sixteen persons to be hanged at Yarmouth, forty at Bury, and others in different parts of the country, to the number of sixty persons. Hopkins used many arts to extort confessions from the suspected, and when these failed he tied their thumbs and great toes together, and threw them into the water. If they floated, they were guilty; if they sank, they were innocent. This method was pursued until some gentleman, indignant at Hopkins's barbarity, tied his thumbs and toes together, and threw him into the water, when he swam, by which expedient the country was soon rid of him. Hopkins is represented in an old engraving as a spare man with a tight-fitting dress, conical hat, and a staff in his hand. He first visited Aldeburgh the day before the execution of an old woman, Mother Lakeland, at Ipswich, on the 8th September, 1645, who, in a pamphlet published after her death, is said to have confessed that she had sold herself to the Devil twenty years before, and had been furnished with three imps, in the forms of two dogs and a mole, by which she had grievously afflicted Mr. Lawrence, Mr. Beal, a maid of Mr. Jennings's, besides other persons in that town.

The following items from the Chamberlain's accounts for 1645–6 will best narrate Hopkins's activity at Aldeburgh :—

"Given Mr. Hopkyns, the 8th September, £2 for a gratuitie, he being in town for finding out witches. One pound to Goody Phillips there for her pains for searching out witches. 13s. 10d. to sundry men for watching days and nights with such as are apprehended for witches. Two pounds more to Mr. Hopkins, the 20th December, for being in town for finding out witches. One pound to widow Phillips, the search-woman. 12s. 8d. paid Mr. Thos. Johnson, that he paid Mr. Skinner's men for fetching widow Phillips. A further sum of £2 for Mr. Hopkyns for a gratuitie for giving evidence against the witches in the jail, the 7th of January. Paid six men to ward at the Sessions and execution for two days and a half, at 12d. per day, and 6d. to drink, all is 15s. 6d. Paid John Pame, eleven shillings for hanging seven witches. Paid Mr. Dannell, £1 for the gallows, and setting them up. For a post to set by the grave of the dead bodies that were hanged, and for burying of them, six shillings. Paid Henry Lawrence, the roper, eight shillings for seven halters, and making the knots. Received of Mr. Newgate, March 13th, 1645, in part for the charge of trying a witch in Aldeburgh, the sum of £4. Received of Mr. Richard Brown by the hands of Mr. Bailiff Johnson, May 25th, 1646, in part, for the charges of trying a witch in Aldeburgh, the sum of £4."

N. F. Hele.　"Notes or Jottings about Aldeburgh,"
pp. 41–3.　Second Edition (1890).

Matthew Hopkins assumed the title of Witch-finder General, and travelling through the counties of Essex, Sussex, Suffolk, Norfolk, and Huntingdon, pretended to discover witches. . . . His principal mode of discovery was to strip the accused persons naked and thrust pins into various parts of their body, to discover the witch's mark, which was supposed to be inflicted by the devil as a sign of his sovereignty, and at which she was also said to suckle her imps. He also practised and stoutly defended the trial by swimming, when the suspected person was wrapped in a sheet, having the great toes and thumbs tied together, and so dragged through a pond or river. If she sank, it was received in favour of the accused; but if the body floated (which must have occurred ten times for once, if it was placed with care on the surface of the water), the accused was condemned, on the principle of King James, who, in treating of this mode of trial, lays down that, as witches have renounced their baptism, so it is just that the element through which the holy rite is enforced should reject them, which is a figure of speech, and no argument. It was Hopkins's custom to keep the poor wretches waking, in order to prevent them from having encouragement from the devil, and, doubtless, to put infirm, terrified, overwatched persons in the next state to absolute madness; and for the same purpose they were dragged about by their keepers till extreme weariness and the pain of blistered feet might form additional inducements to confession.

"Demonology and Witchcraft," by Sir Walter Scott, Bart. London: George Routledge and Sons, 1887, p. 206.

The following were the principal methods employed by Hopkins and his crew in the discovery of witchcraft:—

I. To weigh them against the church Bible; if the suspected person was the heaviest, she was set at liberty.

II. To make them repeat the Lord's Prayer and Apostles' Creed. This no witch was ever able to do correctly.

[These methods were only occasionally used; they were far too humane for the "Witch-finder General" and his satellites.]

III. By swimming, which was the most usual practice. The hands and feet of the suspected were tied together cross-wise, right hand thumb to toe of left foot, and *vice-versâ*; they were wrapped in a sheet or blanket and placed upon their backs in a pond or river. If they sank, they were innocent; if they floated, they were guilty and condemned to the fire.

IV. By pricking. This, the most disgusting of the so-called tests, began by a search for the devil's private mark, noted above as being insensible to pain, into which, when found, large pins were stuck (some three inches long). . . . .

V. By watching, The witch was placed cross-legged, or in some
other uneasy position, upon a chair or table, and kept for four-
and-twenty hours without food. It was supposed that one or other
of her attendant imps would come during that interval and suck
her blood, and as it might come in the shape of a fly, wasp, or moth,
watchers were appointed with special instructions to kill any insect
that might enter. If an insect thus chased escaped, the woman was
guilty—that insect was her familiar; she went to the stake, and
the witch-finder pocketed his twenty shillings.

There is something like poetical justice in the manner in which
Hopkins met his death. His influence slowly decayed, and in a
village in Suffolk the people were disposed to doubt the charge of
witchcraft he had brought against a woman of the place. In proof
he produced a memorandum book, in which he said Satan had
entered the names of all the witches in England, when someone in
the crowd suggested that the possession of such a book was proof
positive of his own traffic with Satan. In spite of his remonstrances,
he was seized and put to his own test. Some say that he floated,
and was summarily executed by the mob ; others that he was
drowned.

J. T. Varden. " E. A. Handbook," for 1885, p. 89.

From the famous Trial of the Essex Witches, arraigned and
condemned at Chelmsford, July 29, 1645, pp. 817-858, I extract
the following :—

"This informant [John Rivet, of Manningtree, Taylor] saith,
That about Christmas last, his wife was taken sicke and lame,
with such violent fits, that this informant verily conceived her
sickness was something more than meerly naturall : whereupon this
informant, about a fortnight since, went to a cunning woman, the
wife of one Hovye, at Hadleigh, in Suffolke, who told this informant
that his wife was cursed by two women, who were neer neighbours
to this informant, the one dwelling a little above his house, and the
other beneath his house, this informant's house standing on the side
of an hill: whereupon he believed his said wife was bewitched by
one Elizabeth Clarke, *alias* Bedingfield, that dwelt above this

informant's house, for that the said Elizabeth's mother and some other of her kinsfolke did suffer death for witchcraft and murther."

Then, later on : " This informant [Richard Edwards, of Manningtree, Gent.] saith, that not long since, about three months to his best remembrance, as he was coming from Eastberryholt in Suffolke, halfe an houre within the evening, within ten score of the middle bridge (according to the desire of the said Elizabeth Clarke, as is declared in the confession of the said Rebecca Weste) this informant's horse started with him, and greatly endangered him ; and he heard something about his horse cry, Ah, ah ! much like the shrieke of a polcat. And this informant saith, That with much difficulty he saved himselfe from being thrown off his horse. All which, this informant reported to his wife and neighbours as soone as he came home."

S. L. G. " Suffolk Notes and Queries," Ipswich Journal. 1877.

The laws against witchcraft were, during the years 1645–6, rigidly enforced in Suffolk, and Rev. John Lewis, who was presented to the Vicarage of Brandeston, in May, 1596, where he lived 50 years, was executed as a wizard. Matthew Hopkins, of Manningtree, the celebrated witch-finder, brought some hundreds to the gallows, and the Parliament highly rewarded him for his services. By order of the Privy Council, commissioners were appointed for the trial of witchcraft, and were often nominated from the Presbyterian Divines. Baxter unfortunately sanctioned the cruelties which Hopkins inflicted on those who were suspected of witchcraft, and thus writes respecting Mr. Lewis :—" Mr. Calamy went along with the judges on the circuit to hear the witches' confessions, and to see there was no fraud or wrong done unto them. I spoke with many understanding, pious, learned, and credible persons that lived in the counties, and some that went to them in the prisons and heard their sad confessions. Among the rest, an old reading parson named Lewis, not far from Framlingham, was one that was hanged, who confessed that he had two imps, and that one of them was always putting him upon doing mischief : and he being near the sea, as he saw a ship under

sail, it moved him to send it to sink the ship: and he consented
and saw the ship sink before him." Sir Walter Scott, from whose
letters on Demonology and Witchcraft the above quotation has been
made, thus writes:—"Notwithstanding the story of his alleged
confession, Mr. Lewis defended himself courageously at his trial,
and was probably condemned rather as a Royalist and malignant
than for any other cause. He showed at the execution considerable
energy, and to secure that the funeral service of the Church should
be said over his body, he read it aloud for himself while on the
road to the gibbet."

J. J. "Suffolk Notes and Queries," Ipswich Journal.

The following, many years since, was copied by me from a manu-
script. I am unable to give the exact title of the book; but as well
as I can remember, it was a History and Description of the Manor of
Brandeston, and of the Church, etc., by a former steward of the
manor :—

"Vicars of Brandeston, Suffolk."—"John Lowes, Instituted 6th
May, 1596, on the Presentation of Charles Seckford, Esquire, was,
after he had been vicar here about 50 years, and 80 years of age,
accused of Witchcraft, put into the Castle Ditch at Framlingham,
for Triall thereof, where he did swim, and so did other old Persons
then put therein, always reputed honest People. . Swimming is no
proof of Witchcraft as to aged Persons, for the Radical moisture,
Juices and Blood, being naturally wasted by Age, the Body is
thereby rend'red lighter than the quantity of Water it occupies, and
consequently must swim. His chief accuser was one Hopkins (who
called himself Witch-finder General, had 20s. of every Parish he went
to, and died miserably). This Rascal kept the poor old Man awake
severall Days and Nights together, in a large Room in the Castle,
till he was delirious and confest (as Witnesses testified) such
familiarity with the Devill, as had such Weight with the Jury
and his Judges (viz.) Serjeant Godcold, Old Calamy, and Fair-
clough, as to condemn him, with 59 more for the like crime, at
St. Edmund's Bury, about the beginning of 1646, altho' he stoutly
maintained his Innocency. And when he came to the place of

Execution, because he would have Christian Buriall, he read the Office himself. But John Revet, Esquire, his Parishioner, and Brian Smith, Dr. in Divinity (afterwards Rector of Rendlesham in the Neighbourhood), who both knew him verie well, altogether acquits him of that crime, as far as they could judge, and verily believed, that Mr. Lowes, being a Litigious Man, made his Parishioners (too tenacious of their customs) very uneasy, so that they were glad to take the opportunity of those Wicked times, to get him hanged, rather than not get rid of him. . . . Allusion is made to him and the Rest in Hudibras, Part II, Canto 3."

> East Anglian. " Suffolk Notes and Queries," Ipswich Journal.

On the left side of Northgate-road [Bury St. Edmunds] is the " Thinghow," a mound which gives name to the Hundred, and which was the ancient place of assembly for the " Thing," a word suggesting the period when Suffolk lay within the " Danelagh." The " Thinghow " was the place of execution till 1766, and the forty persons hanged at Bury in 1644, under the ban of Hopkins, the " witch-finder,"—

> " Who after proved himself a witch,
> And made a rod for his own breech "—

no doubt suffered here.

> Murray. " Handbook for Essex, Suffolk, Norfolk, and Cambridgeshire," p. 134.

Mother Lakeland, of Ipswich, 1645.

In an old tract bearing the title of " The Laws against Witches and Conjurations " is preserved a curious statement purporting to be the confession of a famous witch of Ipswich, known as Mother Lakeland. According to this document, Mother Lakeland sold herself to the devil, who supplied her with three familiars in the shape of two little dogs and a mole. She practised first on her husband, who, after lying long in great misery, died; then on a Mr. Laurence, of Ipswich, and his child, tormenting them to death by her sorceries, all on account of the former asking her for some ten or twelve shillings she owed him. A Mrs. Jennings was also done to death by the mole aforesaid, and Mr. Beale, of Ipswich, suffered much at her hands ; a fine new ship owned by him was burnt before it went to sea, and himself reduced to a mere skeleton by her machinations. This good lady was burnt at Ipswich, Sept. 9th, 1645, and it is said that her latest victim, Beale, began at once to amend, and seemed in a very short time to be in a fair way of recovery.

> J. T. Varden. "East Anglian Handbook for 1885,"
> p. 92.

The Case of Magdalen Holyday.

The county of Suffolk was remarkable for the number of *Witches* which were known to practice their diabolical arts in it. Baxter says he knew more than a *hundred* at one time. . . . The present case is found in a copy of Baxter's " World of Spirits," and was probably preserved for another edition, which did not appear. It is directed to him—

Worthy Sir,—Your last, of the 6th of July, I duly received, and since that, I have inquired further into the business of the possession of *Magdalen Holyday*, maidservant to the Parson of Sax-mundham, Suffolk, as you desired ; you saying, it would be of use to your forthcoming volume, and of which case I informed you, in a letter dated Nov. 1, 1685, and forwarded to you by the Ipswich waggon to the Rose Inn, Smithfield. Now, being myself lately on a visit to my sister's nephew in these parts, a painstaking, honest man, living at Freston, under the Lord Stafford, which village is near to the sea, and not far from the said town of Saxmundham ; I have made due and diligent enquiry thereupon in answer to your pressing entreaties, that I would enrich your next Work on Appari-tions and Witchcrafts with this case ; I here forthwith send it to you, as I have received it from the mouths of many sober, creditable persons in these parts. Witness my hand—Tobias Gilbert, Cord-wainer, No. 2 East Cheap, now dwelling at Freston aforesaid.

" *Magdalen Holyday*, spinster, aged eighteen years, the daughter

of poor honest persons, Phineas and Martha Holyday, of the parish
of Rendham, near Framlingham (as may be seen by the register of
the said parish), was servant-maid to Mr. Simon Jones, minister
of the parish of Saxmondham, with whom she had dwelt for the
space of three years and upwards; and was esteemed by all the
neighbours as a civil, well-behaved young woman, of good conduct
above her years, very decent and frugal in her apparell, modest in
her behaviour, sweet and civil in her speech, and painstaking in her
religion; so that she was well respected of all in the said parish,
young and old. She was also a very fair and comely person, save
only a defect in the colour of her hair, for moderate stature, and
a cheerful disposition; nor was any reproach ever thrown upon
her, save that some few of the *Gospellers* (a party that sprang up in
the reign of Queen Elizabeth, and doth now continue to the great
division of the One Catholic Church) would taunt her, that being
handmaid to a Minister of the Church, she would frequent wakes
and fairs at Whitsuntide, and Saint days and holy days, but they
could not throw anything in her teeth which they would, as she
always went in company with her brother, aunts, or other sober
people of good repute, who could keep the scandal from her door.
Her family did not like Oliver Cromwell nor any of his ordinances,
but were true and faithful to King Charles of blessed memory,
though they were but poor folk. Now Magdalen Holyday had, in
her youth, been touched of the King for the evil when he came
into the associated counties, but since that she had always preserved
her health, so that the rose blush in her cheek, and the milky snow
on her forehead, were known to all. But to come to my story. It
happened on Monday, in Lammas, the year 1672, about noon, as
she was carrying in dinner, no one in the parlour save the parson
and his wife and their eldest daughter, Rebecca, then about to be
married to a worthy and painstaking Gospel Minister, then living
at the parish of Yoxford, in the said county; that on a sudden,
just as she had placed a suet dumpling on the board, that she
uttered a loud shriek, as if she were distraught, and stooping down
as in great pain, said she felt a pricking as of a large *Pin* in the
upper part of her leg; but did not think that any such thing could

1 7

be there. Yet on ungartering her hose, she felt a pin had got there, within the skin yet not drawing blood, nor breaking the skin, nor making any hole or sign, and she could hardly feel the head of it with her finger, and from that time it continued tormenting her with violent and retching pains all the day and night, and this continuing and nothing assuaged, Mistress Jones, by advice of the Minister, sent for the assistance of two able Apothecaries (medici) then dwelling in the said town ; one, a chirurgion of great repute too, who had studied under the famous Hondius at Frankfort ; the other, a real son of Galen, who, on examining the part, and above and below, at sufficient distance, both declared they could see neither " vola, nec vestigium " of the said pin ; but on her constant and confident assertion there was a pin, though it had now time to work itself deeper into the flesh like an insidious enemy, they made an incision, but could find none, only the maid asserted that a few days before, an old woman came to the door and begged a pin of her, and she not giving her one, the said woman muttered something, but she did not suspect her. And now it was time these noted leeches should do something for this afflicted person ; for now she lies in ceaseless torment, both by night and by day, for if she slept, her sleep was troubled with dreams and wicked apparitions : sometimes she saw something like a mole run into her bed, sometimes she saw a naked arm held over her, and so was this poor maid thus tormented by evil spirits, in spite of all Godly prayers and ringing of church bells, etc. But now the doctors took her in hand ; their names Anthony Smith, Gent., and Samuel Kingston, chirurgion to Sir John Rouse, of Henham, Knt. Having taken down the deposition of the said Magdalen Holyday before Mr. Pacey, a pious Justice of the Peace, living at Marlesford, in the said county, upon oath, they then gave to the said Magdalen Holyday the following medicines :—Imprimis, a decoction—ex fuga Dœmonium—of southern wood, mugwort vervain, of which they formed a drink according to Heuftius' Medical Epistles, lib. xii., sec. iv., also following Variola, a physician of great experience at the Court of the Emperor. They also anointed the part with the following embrocation :—Dog's grease well mixed, four ounces ; bear's fat, two ounces ; eight ounces of capon's grease; four and twenty slips of mistletoe, cut in pieces and powdered small with gum of Venice turpentine, put close into a phial, and exposed for nine days to the sun till it formed into a green balsam, with which the said parts were daily anointed for the space of three weeks, during which time, instead of amendment, the poor patient daily got worse, and vomited, not without constant shrieks or grumbling, the following substances:—Paring of nails, bits of spoons, pieces of brass (triangular), crooked pins, bodkins, lumps of red hair, egg-shells broken, parchment shavings. a hen's bone of the leg, one thousand two hundred worms, pieces of glass, bones like the great teeth of a horse, a luminous matter, sal petri (not thoroughly prepared), till at length relief was found, when well nigh given up, when she brought up with violent retching, *a whole row of pins stuck on blew paper!!* After that, these sons of Æsculapius joyfully perceived that their potent drugs had wrought the designed cure—they gave her comfort, that she had subdued her bitter foe, nor up to the present time has she been afflicted in any way; but having married an honest poor man, though well to do in the world, being steward to Sir John Heveningham, she has borne him four healthy children. . . . . Whether this punishment was inflicted by the said old woman, an emissary of Satan, or whether it was meant wholesomely to rebuke her for frequenting wakes, may-dances, and Candlemas fairs, and such like pastimes, still to me remains in much doubt. " Non possum solvere nodum." Sir, your thankful servant, T.G.—*Freston Parish nigh to Saxmondham*; *sent by the carrier.*

P.S.—I hear the physicians followed up their first medicine with castory, and rad. ostrutii and sem. danci, on Forestius' his recommendation.

From a cutting, evidently taken from some Suffolk newspaper (no name or date given) in an interesting collection of various material relating to Suffolk in the possession of Mr. J. Loder, of Woodbridge. Cf. *Gent. Mag. Library*, " Popular Superstitions," pp. 277–280.

Lowestoft Witches, 1664.

Rose Cullender and Amy Duny, of Lowestoft, were tried for witchcraft at Bury St. Edmund's, March 10th, 1664, before the learned and upright Sir Matthew Hale, condemned and executed on the 17th of the same month. They were accused of bewitching certain children, affecting them with strange fits, during which they vomited pins and twopenny nails, and depriving them of the use of their limbs; also bewitching the horses of a cart which accidentally collided with the corner of the house of one of them, so that they died; while for a similar accident another stalwart yeoman found his waggon immovable and himself troubled with bleeding at the nose on his attempting to unload it. The most curious incident in the evidence against them was that the mother of one of the bewitched children consulted a Doctor Jacob, of Yarmouth, concerning its strange condition, and he having some experience in such cases, told her to hang up the blanket in which the child slept by the chimney corner all day, and at night when she put the child to bed to wrap it in the same, and whatever she found therein she was without fear immediately to throw into the fire. She did so, and when she took the blanket down, a great black toad fell from it, which, being caught by a youth in the house and held with the tongs in the fire, *exploded* with a loud noise and disappeared. On the morrow the news was bruited abroad that Amy Duny was in a sad plight, and the mother going to see her found her sitting alone in the house with her face and legs very much scorched and burnt, and scarcely a rag of clothing upon her. Mistress Duny informed her that she might thank her for it, and that she intended to be revenged, for she (the mother) should live to see some of her children dead, while herself should be compelled to go upon crutches. . . . . The learned Sir Thomas Browne, of Norwich, . . . appeared to testify his belief in witchcraft. The prisoners were hanged.

J. T. Varden. "East Anglian Handbook" for 1885, p. 93.

In John Aubrey's "Miscellanies upon the following Subjects," etc. (London, 1721), is the following passage:—" Under the porch of Stanisfield Church in Suffolk, I saw a Tile with a Horse-shoe upon it, placed there for this purpose [to hinder the power of Witches that enter into the House], though one would imagine that Holy Water would alone have been sufficient."

C. S. "Suffolk Notes and Queries," Ipswich Journal.

I may here add that I have seen a horse-shoe nailed on a cottage threshold as a preservative against a witch—the idea being that she could not step over cold iron.

Ed. Moor. "Suffolk Words and Phrases," p. 263.

I send the following extract from an article in an old newspaper, dated 1792, headed "Country News:"—

"Bury, June 20. In the course of an examination relative to a pauper on Wednesday se'nnight before Sir Charles Davers, Bart., and the Rev. John Ord, at the Angel Inn, an old woman of Stanningfield charged another with having called her Witch, which she said had very much disordered her head; but the Justices telling her they could take no cognizance thereof, she on Wednesday last voluntarily submitted to the usual ordeal; at first it was proposed to weigh her against the Church Bible, but the clergyman refused to lend the same, when her husband, brother, and another man tied a rope round her body, and cast her into a horsepond, from whence, as she was found to sink, they dragged her out almost lifeless. On the men being rebuked for this egregious instance of folly, in complying with so extraordinary a request, and particularly the husband, he said that he thought it better to indulge her therein, than to suffer her to destroy herself, which was certain she would have done had she not undergone this trial."

Acton, Middlesex. Charles Ed. Stewart. "Suffolk Notes and Queries," Ipswich Journal.

Witchcraft.—In the 3rd Vol. of the "Proceedings of the Suffolk Institute of Archæology," p. 309, it is stated that a poor unfortunate

1 7 *

witch so late as 1795 "went through the usual sufferings in a pond close to the churchyard of Stanningfield." I am told the ordeal of water took place at the pond on the green called "Hoggage Green" (why so called?); that the name of the witch was "Greygoose," and that she had "six imps—Silcock, Wisky, Turntail, Toby, Tarrain, and Tegg."

> *Buriensis.* Quoted in "Suffolk Notes and Queries," Ipswich Journal, from "The East Anglian," for Sept. 1863.

In July, 1825, a man was "swam for a wizard" at Wickham-Skeith, in Suffolk, in the presence of some hundreds of people. In that parish lives Isaac Stebbings, a little spare man about sixty-seven years old, who obtains a livelihood as a huckster; and hard by his cottage lives a thatcher whose wife is afflicted in mind. In the same parish there happens to be a farmer whose mind is occasionally disturbed. Some one or other put forth the surmise, that these two afflicted persons were bewitched, and Stebbings was spoken of as the "worker of the mischief." Story grew on story; accumulated hearsays were accepted as proof "undeniable." Among other things it was said that the friends of the afflicted woman had recourse to some means recorded in the annals of witchcraft for detecting the devil's agent; and that whilst the operation was going on at night, Stebbings came dancing up to the door. In his denial of this circumstance, Stebbings admitted that he did once call at his neighbour's with mackerel for sale at four o'clock in the morning, before the family were up, and this admission was taken to be as much as he was likely to make. Besides this, the village shoemaker, persisted that one morning, as Stebbings passed two or three times before his house, he could not "make" his wax—the ingredients would neither melt nor mix. Dubbed a wizard beyond all doubt, poor Stebbings, ignorant as his neighbours, and teased beyond bearing. proposed at length of himself the *good* old-fashioned ordeal of "sink or swim." The proposal was readily caught at, and on the following Saturday, at two o'clock, in a large pond, called the *Grimmer*, on Wickham-Green, four men walked into the water with him, and the constable of the parish engaged to attend and keep the peace! The sides of the pond were crowded with spectators—men, women and children. Stebbings had on his breeches and shirt; and when the men had walked with him into the water breast-high, they lifted him up and laid him flat upon his back on the water. Stebbings moved neither hand nor foot, and continued in that position for ten minutes. This was the first trial, and the spectators called out "give him another." Another trial was accordingly given, for the same length of time, and with the same result. "Try him again and dip him under the water," was then the cry. They did so: one of the four men pressed his chest, and down went his head whilst up came his heels; in a word he was like a piece of cork in the water. These trials kept the poor old fellow three-quarters of an hour in the pond, and he came out "more dead than alive." Still, some were not satisfied. Another man, they said, of his age and size, ought to be swam with him. Stebbings agreed even to this, for he was determined to get rid of the imputation, or die. The following Saturday was appointed for the purpose, and a man called Tom Wilden, of Bacton parish, hard by, was named for his companion. The story now got more wind, and hundreds of people from all the neighbouring parishes attended to witness the second ordeal. But in the interval, the clergyman of the parish and the two churchwardens had interfered, and the swimmers were kept away, to the no small vexation and disappointment of the deluded multitude. It is gravely told, that at the very time Stebbings was swum, the afflicted farmer alluded to above was unusually perturbed; he cried out, "I can see the imps all about me; I must frighten them away with my voice;" and his delusion and his noise, as Stebbings did not sink, are put down to his account. To complete the affair, a respectable farmer in a neighbouring parish went, it is said, to some "cunning man," and learnt to a certainty that Stebbings was a wizard. The sum of £3 was paid for this intelligence, and for the assurance that Stebbings should be "killed by inches."

These particulars in *The Times* newspaper of July 19, 1825,

extracted from the *Suffolk Chronicle*, prove the deplorable ignorance
of certain human beings in England.

> "The Everyday Book," by W. Hone, vol. i, p. 942.
> See Forby. "Vocabulary of East Anglia," vol. ii,
> p. 391.

Some years ago, in Berkshire, a young fellow in the militia
gave me a receipt for hurting an enemy, which he had learnt of
a "wise woman" at Aldershot. It was, to take a piece of red
cloth, stick pins in it, and then burn it in a clear fire. I remember
telling this afterwards to a rat-catcher, a genuine Suffolker and a
great crony of mine. He heard me attentively, much as a man
of science might listen to an account of a new discovery in
chemistry; made me repeat the formula, the better to impress it
on his memory; and then "S'help me lucky," he said, "but I'll
try that on my brother, I'ool."

> G. d'A. "Suffolk Notes and Queries," Ipswich Journal.

In the Eastern Counties it is believed that neither a witch nor
a person using charms for any purpose whatever can die without
delivering her secret to another.

> J. T. Varden. "E. A. Handbook," for 1885, p. 96.

Mrs. Mullinger was a strange old woman. People said she had
an evil eye; and if she took a dislike to anyone and looked evilly
at their pigs, then the pigs would fall ill and die. Also, when
she lived next door to another cottage, with only a wall dividing
the two chimneys, if old Mrs. Mullinger sat by her chimney in
a bad temper, no one on the other side could light a fire, try as
they might.

> Francis Hindes Groome. "A Suffolk Parson," Black-
> wood's Edinburgh Magazine. March, 1891, p. 319.

Will, like many other old people in the parish, believed in witchcraft, was himself indeed a "wise man" of a kind. My father

once told him about a woman who had fits. "Ah!" old Will
said, "she've fallen into bad hands." "What do you mean?"
asked my father; and then Will said that years before in Monk
Soham there was a woman took bad just like this one, and "there
weren't but me and John Abbott in the place could get her right."
"What did you do?" said my father. "We two, John and I,
sat by a clear fire; and we had to bile some of the clippin's of
the woman's nails and some of her hair; and when ta biled," he
paused. "What happened?" asked my father; "did you hear
anything?" "Hear anything! I should think we did. When ta
biled, we h'ard a loud shrike a-roarin' up the chimley; and yeou
may depind upon it, she warn't niver bad no more."

Ibid, p. 318.

The "Ancient Fisherman," whose character is pourtrayed in these
stanzas (The invocation by Mrs. J. Cobbold, of Holy Wells, Ipswich),
was . . . once resident in the parish of St. Clement, Ipswich, by
name Thomas Colson, but better known by the appellation of Robinson
Crusoe. . . . He . . . became a fisherman on the Orwell. . . He
was a firm believer in the evil agency of wizards and witchcraft. On
this subject he was by no means uninformed; and a frequent perusal
of the Dæmonology of . . . K. James I, . . . soon confirmed his
belief in these absurd opinions. He appeared also to have read
"Glanvil's Saducismus Triumphans" with considerable attention. . .
His mind was so haunted with the dreams of charms and enchant-
ments, as to fancy that he was continually under the influence of
these mischievous tormentors. His arms and legs, nay, almost his
whole body, was encircled with the bones of horses, rings, amulets
and characts, verses, words, etc., as spells and charms to protect him
against their evil machinations. On different parts of his boat was to
be seen the "horse shoe nailed," that most effective antidote against
the power of witches. When conversing with him, he would describe
to you that he saw them hovering about his person, and endeavouring,
by all their arts, to punish and torment him. . . . However powerful
and effective his charms might be to protect him from the agency of
evil spirits, they did not prove sufficiently operative against the

dangers of storm and tempest. For being unfortunately driven on the Ooze by a violent storm on the 3rd October, 1811, he was seen and earnestly importuned to quit his crazy vessel; but relying on the efficacy of his charms, he obstinately refused; . . . and poor Robinson sunk to rise no more.

"The Suffolk Garland," 1818, p. 8.

Exorcism by Fire.—A woman I knew forty-three years ago had been employed by my predecessor to take care of his poultry. At the time I came to make her acquaintance she was a bedridden toothless crone, with chin and nose all but meeting. She did not discourage in her neighbours the idea that she knew more than people ought to know, and had more power than others had. Many years before I knew her it happened one spring that the ducks, which were a part of her charge, failed to lay eggs. . . . She at once took it for granted that the ducks had been bewitched. This misbelief involved very shocking consequences, for it necessitated the idea that so diabolical an act could only be combated by diabolical cruelty. And the most diabolical act of cruelty she could imagine was that of baking alive in a hot oven one of the ducks. And that was what she did. The sequence of thought in her mind was that the spell that had been laid on the ducks was that of preter-naturally wicked wilfulness; that this spell could only be broken through intensity of suffering, in this case death by burning; that the intensity of the suffering would break the spell in the one roasted to death; and that the spell broken in one would be altogether broken, that is, in all the ducks. . . . Shocking, however, as was this method of exorcising the ducks, there was nothing in it original. Just about a hundred years before, everyone in the town and neighbourhood of Ipswich had heard, and many had believed, that a witch had been burnt to death in her own house at Ipswich by the process of burning alive one of the sheep she had bewitched. It was curious, but it was as convincing as curious, that the hands and feet of this witch were the only parts of her that had not been incinerated. This, however, was satisfactorily explained by the fact that the four feet of the sheep, by which it had been suspended over the fire, had not been destroyed in the flames that had consumed its body.

Some materials for the "History of Wherstead," by F. Barham Zincke. Ipswich: 1887, p. 168.

1744.—The last of them [*i.e.* the "Ipswich Witches"], one Grace Pett, laid her hand heavily on a farmer's sheep, who, in order to punish her, fastened one of the sheep in the ground and burnt it, except the feet, which were under the earth. The next morning Grace Pett was found burnt to a cinder, except her feet. Her fate is recorded in the "Philosophical Transactions" as a case of spontaneous combustion.

"Handbook for Essex, Suffolk, etc. Murray: p. 109. See Forby, vol. ii, p. 396.

A Wizard's Curse.—Many years ago a man told me that a row of plum-trees that had in his time grown in a garden in this parish — they had been parallel to and not far from the road —had been cursed by a wizard. He had been overheard, while passing them, to mutter his curse. After that they never bore any more fruit, and gradually died out, so that at the time my informant mentioned to me the occurrence there was not one of them remaining. . . . I ridiculed to my informant the idea that these plum-trees had been cursed, and that any curse could have any such effect. He earnestly deprecated my ridicule with the remark, "You do not know, Sir, what may come of what you are saying. These people have obtained very great power. Mischief may be laid on you for what you are now saying. One ought to be careful not to anger, it is better not to speak about, these people."

Zincke, p. 173.

A Wizard's Familiars.—Over forty years ago the occupier of a farm of about 400 acres, and who was also a churchwarden, told me that in his younger days—he was then about sixty-five—on his entering the room of a wizard with whom he was acquainted—the wizard's name was Winter, and he resided at Aldborough ; the name of the man and

his place of residence were given in the belief that they were all but
unanswerable vouchers for the truth of the story—he saw on the
table before the wizard some half-dozen imps. They were black, the
colour of the white man's devil. In form and size they were something between rats and bats, the most mischievous and hideous of
English animals. They were twittering to the wizard : they could
not be allowed human voice. As soon as my informant entered the
room they were ordered to vanish : the mysteries of iniquity must not
be exhibited to honest men. They obeyed this order by gliding down
to the floor : they could not have the same modes of locomotion as
God's creatures. They then vanished through the floor : solid substances, impermeable to God's creatures, were permeable to them.
I take it for granted that the narrator believed he had seen all this.
. . . . He believed . . . . that his cows and his calves had been bewitched, when they were only suffering from natural ailments, and
he . . . . had recourse to nailing up a horse-shoe over his cow-house,
and to drawing lines and crosses, and circles and triangles in the dust
before the door, which figures he was persuaded it was impossible for
any witch or wizard to step over . . . . he believed that one of his
ploughmen—the man whom he suspected of having bewitched his
cows and calves—had been seen following his plough, not on his feet,
but on his head.

                                                        Ibid. p. 172.

My father, who died several years ago at the age of 85 . . .
still believed in witchcraft. I have as a boy been enraptured by
his tales . . . especially of an old woman who kept a small shop,
and resided on the shore by the Old Green Yard, and whom he
and most of the residents had no doubt bewitched people. He
once called upon a friend of his residing in Albion Street, and on
enquiry as to the health of himself and family, was told by his
friend that his daughter Bessie was very queer, and no doubt
bewitched by the old woman referred to, and that he intended in
the evening to prove it by taking some blood from his daughter,
with part of her hair and nails, etc., and simmer them in a saucepan
over the fire until the ingredients were consumed, the belief being

that as they were consumed so would the life of the witch also
pass away. He left the man preparing his test, and in the morning
called to know the result. After my father left he had placed
the saucepan on the fire, containing the blood, etc., and had been
stirring the ingredients some time, when he heard a great noise
in the cellar, followed by a knocking at the front door; and upon
going to the door, he found the old woman suspected, who, after
making some frivolous remark, bade him good-night and went away.
The mistake made was in going to the door. Had he kept on
with his experiment, the result would have been that as the
ingredients were consumed, so would the old woman have perished.

N.S. "Suffolk Notes and Queries," Ipswich Journal.

Suffolk Superstition.—At an inquest held at Fressingfield, on the
body of a child named Hammond, aged eleven weeks, daughter of
a labourer, the father and mother stated that they believed the
death of the child was due to the witchcraft of Mrs. Corbyn, the
child's step-grandmother. This woman died a few hours before
the child, and stated that the infant would not live long after her.
The child was taken out, and the father stated that he saw smoke
issue from its perambulator, and that she died upon being taken
home, the mother stating that it was hot and dry and smelt of
brimstone. The medical evidence went to show that death was
due to shock caused by the external application of some irritant,
and the jury, in returning a verdict in accordance with the medical
evidence, said there was not sufficient evidence to show the nature
of the irritant. George Corbyn said he was of opinion his late
wife had the powers of a witch, and he always tried to do what
she wanted in consequence.

Sunday Times, 13th April, 1890.

From the Churchwarden's Account Books, Woodbridge (St. Mary's)
1592–1685 :—" 1595. Item. Paid to John Henlington for making
a place upon the ' pillario ' for the witches to stand on . . . 3d."

From Mr. Redstone.

TRIAL OF AMY DUNY AND ROSE CULLENDER, THE
LOWESTOFT WITCHES.

Three of the parties above-named, viz., Anne Durent, Susan
Chandler, and Elizabeth Pacy, were brought to Bury to the
Assizes and were in a reasonable good condition : but that Morning
they came into the Hall to give Instructions for the drawing of
their Bills of Indictments, the Three Persons fell into strange and
violent fits, screeking out in a most sad manner, so that they could
not in any wise give any Instructions to the Court who were the
cause of their Distemper. And although they did after some
certain space recover out of their fits, yet they were every one
of them struck Dumb, so that none of them could speak neither
at that time nor during the Assizes until the Conviction of the
supposed Witches.

[Here follows the evidence of Dorothy Durent, the substance
of which has been given already.]

II. As concerning Elizabeth and Deborah Pacy, the first of the
age of Eleven Years, the other of the age of Nine Years, or thereabouts : as to the Elder, she was brought into the Court at the
time of the Instructions given to draw up the Indictments, and
afterwards at the time of Tryal of the said Prisoners, but could
not speak one Word all the time, and for the most part she remained
as one wholly senseless as one in a deep sleep, and could move
no part of her body. . . . After the said Elizabeth had lain a
long time on the Table in the Court she came a little to herself
and sate up, but could neither see nor speak, but was sensible of
what was said to her . . . and by the direction of the Judg, Amy
Duny was privately brought to Elizabeth Pacy, and she touched
her hand ; whereupon the Child without so much as seeing her,
for her eyes were closed all the while, suddenly leaped up, and
catched Amy Duny by the hand, and afterwards by the face ;
and with her Nails scratched her till Blood came, and would by
no means leave her till she was taken from her, and afterwards
the Child would still be pressing towards her, and manifesting
signs of anger conceived against her.

Deborah, the younger Daughter, was held in such extream manner, that her Parents wholly despaired of her life, and therefore could not bring her to the Assizes.

The Evidence which was given concerning these Two Children was to this Effect :—Samuel Pacy, a merchant of Leystoff aforesaid (a man who carried himself with much soberness during the Tryal, from whom proceeded no words either of Passion or Malice, though his Children were so greatly Afflicted), Sworn and Examined, Deposeth, That his younger Daughter, Deborah, upon Thursday the Tenth of October last, was suddenly taken with a Lameness in her Leggs, so that she could not stand, neither had she any strength in her Limbs to support her, and so she continued until the Seventeenth day of the same Month, which day being fair and Sunshiny, the Child desired to be carryed on the East part of the House to be set upon the Bank which looketh upon the Sea ; and whil'st she was sitting there Amy Duny came to this Deponent's House to buy some Herrings, but being denyed she went away discontented, and presently returned again, and was denyed, and likewise the third time and was denyed as at first, and at her last going away, she went away grumbling; but what she said was not perfectly understood. But at the very same instant of time, the said Child was taken with most violent fits, feeling most extream pain in her Stomach like the Pricking of Pins, and Shrieking out in a most dreadful manner like unto a Whelp and not like a Sensible Creature. . . . A Doctor of Physic . . . being come, he saw the Child but could not conjecture . . . what might be the cause of the Child's Affliction. And this Deponent farther saith, that by reason of the circumstances afore- said, and in regard Amy Duny is a Woman of an ill Fame, and commonly reported to be a *Witch* and *Sorceress*, and for that the said Child in her fits would cry out of Amy Duny as the cause of her Malady, and that she did affright her with the Apparitions of her Person (as the Child in the intervals of her fits related) he this Deponent did suspect the said Amy Duny for a Witch, and charged her with the injury and wrong to his Child, and caused her to be set in the Stocks on the Twenty-eighth of the

same October, and during the time of her continuance there, one
Alice Letteridge and Jane Buxton demanding of her (as they also
Affirmed in Court upon their Oathes) what should be the reason
of Mr. Pacy's Child's Distemper ? telling her, That she was
suspected to be the cause thereof, she replyed, *Mr. Pacy keeps a
great stir about his Child, but let him stay until he hath done as
much by his Children as I have done by mine.* And being further
examined, what she had done by her Children, she answered,
*That she had been fain to open her Child's Mouth with a Tap to
give it Victuals.*

. . . . Within two days . . . the eldest daughter, Elizabeth, fell
into extream fits, insomuch that they could not open her mouth
to give her breath, to preserve her Life, without the help of a Tap
which they were enforced to use; and the younger Child was in
like manner Afflicted. . . . And further the said Children . . .
would severally complain That Amy Duny (together with one other
Woman whose person and Cloathes they described) did thus Afflict
them, their Apparitions appearing before them . . . and sometimes
they would cry out, saying *There stands* Amy Duny, *and there*
Rose Cullender, the other Person troubling them.

Their fits were various, sometimes they would be lame on one
side of their Bodies, sometimes on the other; sometimes a soreness
over their whole Bodies. . . . At other times they would be restored
to the perfect use of their Limbs, and deprived of their Hearing;
at other times of their Sight . . . once wholly . . . of their Speech
for Eight days together. . . . Upon the recovery to their Speech
they would cough extreamly, and bring up . . . crooked pins and
a Two-penny nail with a very broad head. . . . This Deponent
would cause them to Read some Chapters in the New Testament.
Whereupon . . . they would read till they came to the Name of
Lord, or Jesus, or Christ; and then before they could pronounce
either of the said Words they would fall into their fits. But when
they came to the Name of Satan, or Devil, they would clap their
Fingers upon the Book, crying out, *This bites, but makes me speak
right well.*

. . . And further, the said children . . . would tell, how that

Amy Duny and Rose Cullender would appear before them holding their Fists at them, threatning, *That if they related either what they saw or heard, that they would Torment them Ten times more than ever they did before.*

[The children are sent to Yarmouth to their Aunt Margaret Arnold, who gives evidence of "their raising at several times at least Thirty Pins in her presence," when she had carefully taken all pins out of their reach. She continues :]

At some times the children (only) would see things run up and down the House in the appearance of Mice, and one of them suddenly snapt one with the Tongs, and threw it into the fire, and it screeched out like a Rat.

At another time the younger Child . . . went out of Doors to take a little fresh Air, and presently a little thing like a Bee flew upon her Face, and would have gone into her mouth, whereupon the Child ran . . . into the House again, screeking out in a most terrible manner . . . the Child fell into her Swooning Fitt, and at last with much pain she vomited up a Two-penny Nail with a broad Head . . . and being demanded how she came by this Nail? She answered, *That the Bee brought this Nail and forced it into her Mouth.*

At other times, the elder child declared unto this Deponent that during the time of her Fitts, she saw Flies come unto her, and bring with them in their Mouths crooked Pins. . . . At another time she said *she saw a Mouse*, and she crept under the Table looking after it, and at length she put something in her Apron, saying *she had caught it* ; and immediately she ran to the Fire and threw it in, and there did appear unto this Deponent, like the flashing of Gunpowder, though she confessed she saw nothing in the Child's Hand. . . . At another time the Younger Daughter being recovered out of her Fitts declared that Amy Duny *had been with her, and that she tempted her to Drown herself, and to cut her Throat or otherwise destroy herself.*

At another time in their Fitts they both of them cryed out against *Rose Cullender* and *Amy Duny*, complaining against them : *Why do not you come yourselves, but send your Imps to torment us ?*

Edmund Durent, father of Ann, one of the bewitched children, bears witness that his wife refused to sell herrings to Rose Cullender, who "returned in a discontented manner." Soon after his daughter Ann was afflicted with pain in her Stomach, swooning fits, and "vomiting up divers Pins." She declared that during her fits she saw "the Apparition of Rose Cullender," who threatened to torment her.

Diana Bocking testifies to the same symptoms in her daughter Jane, who likewise complains of Rose Cullender and Amy Duny.

Mary Chandler, Mother of Susan, another of the children bewitched, bears testimony to a Warrant against Rose Cullender and Amy Duny being granted by Sir Edmund Bacon, Bt.; the two women accused would confess nothing, and Sir Edmund gave order that they should be searched, appointing Mary Chandler and five others for this office. Whereupon they discovered upon Rose Cullender the Devil's mark. After which Mary Chandler's daughter Susan, aged eighteen, complained of the Apparition of Rose Cullender, fell "extream sick," "vomited up divers crooked pins," and was stricken dumb and blind in turns. The said Susan Chandler when produced in Court, and asked what she could say against either of the Prisoners, "fell into her fits, screeking out in a miserable manner, crying *Burn her, burn her.*"

John Soam, yeoman, of Lowestoft, bears witness that one of his carts having "wrenched the window of Rose Cullender's house," "she came out in a great rage and threatned" him. His other carts went to and fro safely, as usual, but this one after it was loaded was overturned twice or thrice that day, and finally trying to bring it through "the Gate which leadeth out of the Field into the Town" it stuck fast, and they were "inforced to cut down the Post of the Gate to make the Cart pass through, although they could not perceive that the Cart did of either side touch the Gate-posts." After which, when the Cart was brought home into the Yard they could not get it near to the place where they should unload the corn, and when they attempted to unload "at a great distance" they found it so hard a task that others came to assist them; whereupon "their Noses burst forth a-bleeding," and they left it alone until the following morning, when they had no difficulty in unloading it.

Robert Sherringham testifies that about two years since the axletree of his cart touched Rose Cullender's house. She threatned that " his Horses should suffer for it." Shortly after " all those Horses, being four in Number, died ; " since which he had suffered great losses " by the suddain dying of his other Cattle," and by a " Lameness in his Limbs," and by an affliction of Lice, so that " in conclusion he was forced to burn all his Clothes, being two suits of Apparel, and then was clean from them."

Richard Spencer bore witness that Amy Duny had said in his house *That the Devil would not let her rest until she were revenged on one Cornelius Sandeswell's wife*, etc.

Several Gentlemen—Mr. Sergeant Keeling, and " an ingenious person " who objected that the " children might counterfeit this their Distemper," were " unsatisfied " with the Evidence ; upon which, an experiment to see whether her afflicted children recognised blindfold Amy Duny's touch, having failed, Lord Cornwallis, Sir Edmund Bacon, Mr. Sergeant Keeling and others openly protested " that they did believe the whole transaction of this business was a meer imposture." But Mr. Pacy's arguments, and those of the learned Dr. Brown, of Norwich, prevailed. Sir Matthew Hale summed up against the prisoners, who were condemned to be hanged. " They were much urged to confess but would not." Mr. Pacy affirmed of the afflicted children, " That within less than half an hour after the *Witches* were Convicted, they were all of them Restored and slept well that night."]

> A Tryal of Witches at the Assizes Held at Bury St. Edmonds for the Cy of Suffolk ; on the 10 March 1664 Before Sir Matthew Hale Kt. Taken by a Person then attending the Court. London : Printed for W. Shrewsbery at the Bible in Duck Lane 1682.

The following are extracts from a little book which I have recently seen, headed, " Merlinvs Anglicvs Jungor. or the English

Merlin revived, or a Mathematicall prediction upon the affairs of the *English* Commonwealth, and of all or most Kingdoms of Christendom, this present year, 1644."

They do not seem to be *predictions*, but are narrated, it will be observed, as *facts*. . . . The Author of the work is one—"Lilly, student in astrologie."—E.

An innumerable company of Spiders seen marching up one of the Streets at Bury, in Suffolk, Sep. 6, 1660.

At St. Edmund's Bury, in Suffolk, Sept. 6, 1660, in the middle of the Broad Street, there were got together an innumerable company of Spiders of a redish colour, the spectators judged them to be so many as would have filled a Peck; these Spiders marched together and in a strange kind of order, from the place where they were first discovered, towards one Mr. Duncomb's house, a member of the late Parliament, and since Knighted; and as the people passed the street, or came near the spiders, to look upon so strange a sight, they would shun the people, and kept themselves together in a body till they came to the said Duncomb's house, before whose door there are two great Posts, there they staied, and many of them got under the door into the house, but the greatest part of them, climbing up the posts, spun a very great web presently from the one post to the other, and then wrapt themselves in it in two very great parcels that hung down near to the ground, which the servants of the house at last perceiving, got dry straw and laid it under them, and putting fire to it by a suddain flame consumed the greatest part of them, the number of those that remained were not at all considerable; all the use that the Gentleman made of this strange accident, so far as we can learn, is only this, that he believes they were sent to his house by some Witches.

"East Anglian," or "Notes and Queries," ed. by
S. Tymms, vol. iii, p. 57.

1694.] Mother Mummings of Hartis in Suffolk was tried before the Lord Chief Justice Holt at Bury. Many things were deposed concerning her spoiling of work and hurting cattle and that several persons upon their death-beds had complained that she killed them. She threatened her landlord that his nose should lie upward in the churchyard before the next Saturday and before that day he died. She was charged with having an imp like a pole-cat. A person swore that one night passing her cottage he saw her take two imps, one black and another white, out of her basket. She was acquitted.

Hollingsworth's "History of Stowmarket," p. 172.

An old woman used to frequent Stow and she was a witch. If as she was walking any person went after her and drove a nail into the print-mark which her foot left in the dust, she then could not move a step further until it was extracted. The same effects followed from driving a knife well into the ground through the footprint.

Ibid. p. 247.

The most famous man in these parts as a wizard was old Winter of Ipswich. My father was in early life apprentice to him and after that was servant to Major Whyte who lived in Stowupland at Sheepgate Hall. A farmer lost some blocks of wood from his yard and consulted Winter about the .thief. By mutual arrangement Winter spent the night at the farmer's house, and set the latter to watch, telling him not to speak to anybody he saw. About twelve a labourer living near came into the wood-yard and hoisted a block on his shoulder. He left the yard and entered the meadow, out of which lay a style into his own garden. And when he got into the field he could neither find the style nor leave the field. And round and round the field he had to march with the heavy block on his shoulder, affrighted, yet not able to stop walking, until ready to die with exhaustion, the farmer and Winter watching him from the window, until from pure compassion Winter went up to him, spoke, dissolved the charm, and relieved him from his load.—*Sexton.*

1 8 *

Ibid.

A plan for discovering and punishing a Witch.—" When you have good reason to believe that you have been bewitched, get a frying-pan; pull a hair out of your head, and lay it in the pan; cut one of your fingers and let some of your blood fall on the hair. Then hold the pan over the fire until the blood begins to boil and bubble. You may then expect the witch to come and knock at your door three times, wanting to borrow something, and hoping to make you talk. But you must hold your peace. If you utter a word, you will still be more bewitched : if you refuse to speak, you will so work upon the witch's blood as to cause her death ; and then you will be set free."

I obtained this information in a cottage not far from Beccles towards the end of last year.

W. "The East Anglian," edited by S. Tymms, vol. iv, p. 280, 1869.

The Evil Eye.—A nurse of my own—an aged Papist—used to be very angry at encomia on my children ; and I think I have a recollection of her spitting, in cases of apprehended emergency.

Ed. Moor. "Oriental Fragments," p. 326.

I have myself been one of a gang of urchins who nailed a donkey shoe . . . under the threshold of a poor old woman who had the reputation of being suspected of sorcery. We fancied it would avert the exercise of her craft, by confining her all night within doors; as witches cannot cross iron.

Ibid. p. 455.

. . . We have scarcely a town in *Suffolk* of a thousand inhabitants without a fortune-teller; who is, less and less, however, also consulted in the case of stolen goods, and on other occasions.

Ibid. p. 519.

Also published by Llanerch:

OLD SCOTTISH CUSTOMS
W. J. Guthrie

COUNTY FOLKLORE:
ORKNEY & SHETLAND
G. F. Black

COUNTY FOLKLORE:
NORTHUMBERLAND
M. C. Balfour

LEGENDS FROM RIVER AND MOUNTAIN
Carmen Silva, Queen of Roumania

THE FOLKLORE OF PLANTS
T. F. Thiselton Dyer

THE FOLKLORE OF THE ISLE OF MAN
A. W. Moore

THE DAWN OF THE WORLD:
THE MEWAN INDIANS OF CALIFORNIA
C. Hart Merriam

BRITIAN'S LIVING FOLKLORE
Roy Palmer

For a complete list of c.200 small-press editions and
facsimile reprints, write to Llanerch Publishers,
Felinfach, Lampeter, Dyfed, SA48 8PJ.